Ukulele in 5 Days
How to Play Ukulele For Beginners

Frederick Johnson

Copyright © 2019 Frederick Johnson

All rights reserved.

Ukulele Chords Reference Guide

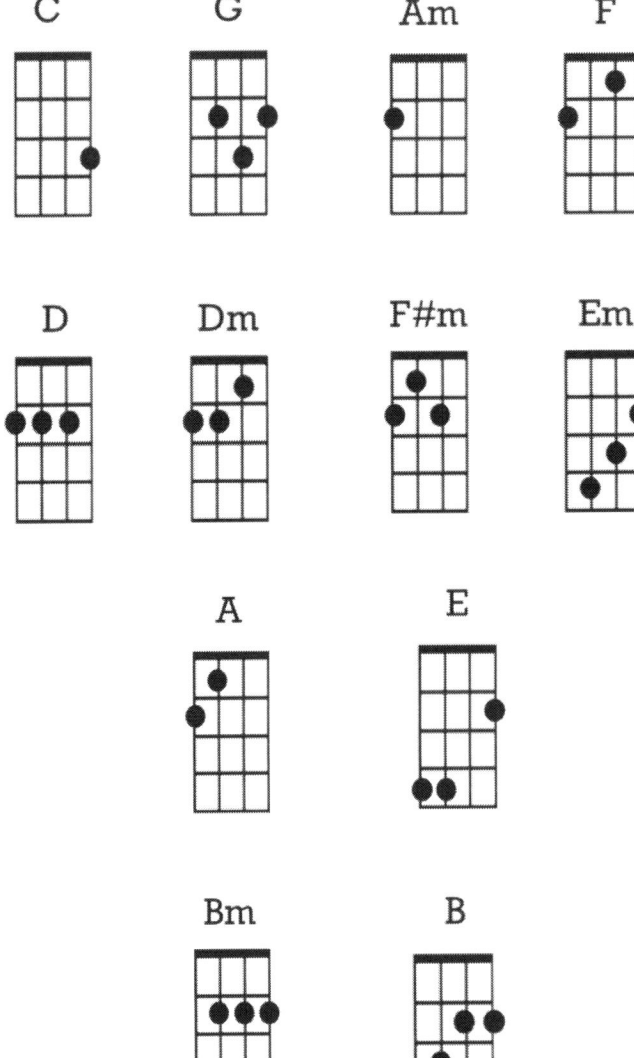

COURSE CONTENTS:

1. **Introduction:** The 5 Day Challenge & Overview (1)

2. **Day One:** Tuning Up & Tabs (11)

3. **Day Two:** Your First Melodies (23)

4. **Day Three:** Chords & Progressions (29)

5. **Day Four:** Important Techniques (43)

6. **Day Five:** Picking & Strumming (73)

7. **Applying Your Knowledge**: Practice Songs (80)

UKULELE IN 5 DAYS

How to Play Ukulele For Beginners

Introduction

Welcome to the '**Ukulele in 5 Days**' introductory guide to the ukulele. This book is an extensive crash course in playing ukulele designed to help you speed up your learning and grasp all the essentials in just 5 days. In order to succeed, you will need to follow each lesson and exercise per day and practice as recommended. It is indeed possible to achieve some degree of affluence of playing within the 5 days so long as you put in the time and effort. Each day is a separate chapter which will cover one new important technique or concept when starting out on the ukulele. You will get out only what you put in and no book will be a magic solution. Nevertheless, we believe that this book which is the first of its kind, is the most thorough and effective for players looking to get a head start on the ukulele from the very first day.

Let's take a look at what will be covered in this book.

Overview

Day One: Tuning Up & Tablature

On the very first day, you will be taught how to tune your instrument accurately and avoid slip ups when doing so. Ensuring that your ukulele remains in perfect tuning is a mundane but pivotal starting point to being a great musician. The second aspect of ukulele playing which will be covered on day one, is tablature. Tablature is used by players of all fretted stringed instruments and is the ukulele equivalent of sheet music.

Day Two: Your First Melodies

We understand that you want to get going as quickly as possible on the ukulele so we kept all the boring housekeeping stuff to day one. On the second day, provided that you have got the hang of tabs, you'll be taught your first melodies. Your musical journey truly begins here.

Day Three: Chords & Progressions

On day three, chords will be taught. In most ukulele guides on the market, chords and progressions are typically taught before tabs and melodies. However, using data from students and monitoring ukulele progress over the years, we have found that chords are best taught after tabs because they involve multiple notes and if you know how to read tablature and how to position your fingers, the chances that chords will stick in your muscle memory are higher if taught afterwards.

Day Four: Important Techniques

On day four, we will have assumed that you have understood tablature and chords. This point must be emphasised because day four will take you to the next level of ukulele playing. These techniques sharpen your playing, involve fun little things you can throw in to make you sound more professional and teach you better musicianship.

Day Five: Picking & Strumming

On day five, you will be introduced to strumming patterns and how to pick the ukulele correctly. This day is again a fine tuning of previously acquired knowledge but will significantly aid you in advancing on the ukulele.

Now that an overview of the book's contents has been provided, let's get started and jump right in. Here's a vital question:

Do you understand your instrument well enough?

We begin with an index of the A-Z of the ukulele.

What is a ukulele?

Many falsely believe that the ukulele is related to the guitar and therefore is part of the guitar family. Others believe that the ukulele is a stand alone instrument whereby it is unique as a construction and no other instruments like it exist. This is also a false misconception.

The truth is that the ukulele is a family of instruments. The uke comes in four sizes: soprano, concert, tenor and baritone. With the increase in demand for stringed instrument production and with advances in recent luthier technology, new hybrids have also emerged such as the guitarlele which is a six string ukulele. This instrument was designed to help guitarists make an easy transition to the ukulele without actually having to learn the ukulele since the instrument has the same intonation as a guitar but tuned a fifth higher. The bass ukulele is another such hybrid. Nevertheless, the chances are that if you're starting the ukulele, you own a soprano since this is the most common kind. **Psst… we think it's the best kind too.**

So let us now take a look at the different parts of the ukulele and what each component is for. Take notes and quiz yourself on the different parts. Knowing your instrument and each element of it will make you a better ukulele player in the long run. It'll help you to pick out your next ukulele as you will better understand what each part in for. In turn, you'll know how to identify good quality.

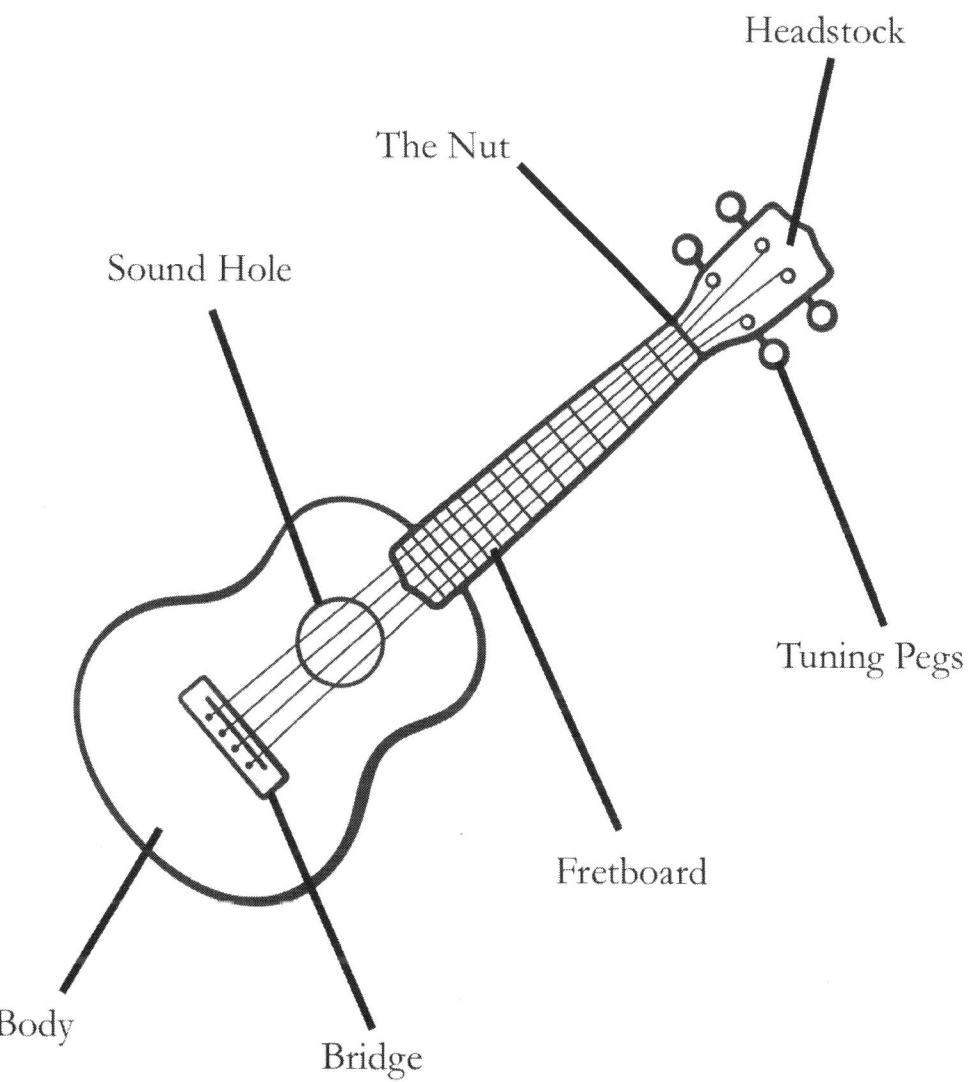

Index
---

1. Headstock

The function of the headstock is to contain the tuning pegs and to balance the ukulele's weight appropriately for an overall accurate intonation.

The headstock is a fragile part of the instrument which you should avoid knocking or hitting at all costs. This point cannot be emphasised enough. Since ukuleles are delicate in that they are smaller than most stringed instruments and have a tighter neck and string tension, even a single heavy knock can cause severe or even permanent damage to the instrument. Such damage can vary from your ukulele no longer staying in tune to a dented neck or even fret and nut problems. Any of these will cost you a lot of money, especially since ukulele repair is a niche field which not all guitar luthiers may be able to pull off successfully. It's best to take precautionary measures and look after your instrument. Purchase a gig bag or case for all transportation.

2. Tuning Pegs

There are four tuning pegs on the ukulele, one for each string. Ukulele tuning pegs are extremely sensitive and so when you are tuning your instrument, especially if you got your instrument new with no setup and loose strings, be extremely cautious as ukulele strings snap HARD if you tune incorrectly and are careless. Tune each peg slowly, turning them progressively - never in quick motions. Since guitars have longer necks than ukuleles, you can afford to tune in swift motions. Ukuleles are smaller and have a shorter distance between the strings and the headstock. Therefore, they tighten quickly. Bear this in mind when first tuning your new instrument.

3. Nut

The nut is often overlooked and some players do not take into consideration just how pivotal this little bit of material really is. The nut is the linking point between the strings, bridge and headstock. It contains four individual slits where the strings sit on. Damage to the nut is as bad as damage to the headstock, if not worse. What you must appreciate as a ukulele player is that while the nut seems futile, those individually spaced slits have been measured apart in a precise way down to the last millimetre. It is actually one of the most strenuous and laborious aspects of the craftsmanship that goes into fabrication of the instrument. When replacing strings, take your time and if you are ever unsure, have them replaced by your local music shop. Better to be safe than sorry.

4. Fretboard

The fretboard is the actual part of the instrument that your notation is played on. If you are right-handed, your left hand navigates this part of the ukulele. Ensure the frets (individually lined notes) are not sharp and are smooth. If there are any issues, make sure to address them professionally before playing as injuries are frequent in poorly constructed and set up ukuleles. Most guitar stores will be able to sort out minor issues. The fretboard sits on the neck which your hand grasps as you play.

5. Soundhole

The sound hole is where sound emits out of the instrument when played. On acoustic guitars, it's where many people accidentally drop their picks into ('***plectrum***' for our lovely British readers). Nonetheless, be sure that nothing is inside the sound hole as this can impair performance and the overall sound of your ukulele.

6. Strings

Let's now talk about the strings of the ukulele. Similar to classical guitars, ukuleles use nylon or gut strings. We will talk specifically about the tuning of the ukulele in the next section of the book. Be aware that your strings should never feel too tight agains the fretboard of the ukulele. There should be an ease where you are able to press down on each fret and bend the strings a little bit. A maintenance tip is to purchase a guitar cleaning kit. These are inexpensive and usually contain conditioner. Keeping your strings clean is essential for hygiene and a crisp sounding instrument. Alternatively, use a duster and dab a small amount of water on a tea towel to regularly clean your fretboard and strings.

7. Bridge

The bridge is what holds the strings in place on the opposite end of the ukulele to the headstock. Don't mess around with this part of the ukulele as much like the other components which involve maintaining correct string tension, it is extremely delicate. You might note that the strings are tied in a knot on the bridge and unlike guitars, there are no pinned 'slots' in the bridge where you can insert strings into easily. This means that changing strings is not something you should try at home unless you are proficient in ukulele string replacement. Ask a guitar or music shop to do this for you when you do eventually buy new strings.

8. Body

Finally, the most prominent feature of your ukulele: its body. Look after it and ensure to dust it from time to time. Dust culminates a lot on the body's outer rim, the headstock and on top of the strings. Just like with any part of the instrument, ensure no physical damage occurs on it and love your instrument like you love any other personal expensive property.

Day One: Tuning Up & Tabs

Welcome to your first day playing the ukulele. Hopefully you're pumped to get playing but this first day might not be as exciting as the others. This is because there is a lot of theory to cover but bear with us! The investment of time that you make now will pay off tomorrow.

Tuning Up

Let me ask you a straight forward question: how many times have you listened to someone play an instrument and it sounded simply terrible? Most of you will be able to answer with confidence. Truth is, that musician probably was playing the right notes and maybe was even a decent musician. What let them down was that their instrument was out of tune. Many debutants seem to think that it's the music that will make an instrument sound good. That's only partly true. Half of what makes a ukulele music sound audible is whether or not the instrument is in perfect tune. Emphasis must be placed on 'perfect' tune. I have come across many beginners who tune approximately to a note but as you develop on your musical journey, you'll find that your ears will become more critical. However, this is a 5 day guide so we are urging you **right now** to take a critical approach.

Tune your ukulele perfectly and do not settle for approximations as so many players do. Believe us when we say that this will make you stand out from other players of your ability.

As we have established: the key to all good performance is a well tuned ukulele. Your tuning abilities will become increasingly more accurate as you progress but from the outset, ensure that you are tuning your ukulele with as much precision as you can and not estimating the note. If you use an online tuner, listen to the note over and over and make absolutely sure your strings are alined with those notes.

So what is ukulele tuning?

Ukulele tuning is similar to other four stringed instruments but is very unique as the second string (the C string) is lower in pitch than the other strings. This is rare in stringed fretted instruments.

Another vital thing is that you remember to tune your instrument before the start of every practice session. Don't assume that because you tuned your ukulele relatively recently that it'll still be in tune. It won't. Even if you own a $1000 instrument, you need to remember to tune it. If that's not reason enough, tuning your ukulele increases it's longevity as the string tension remains healthy and the condition of the nut and bridge is most likely to stand a greater chance in the long run. Respect your instrument, your musicianship and your listeners.

Ukulele tuning looks like this:

G   C   E   A

In tablature form (which we will look at very shortly), it looks like this:

```
T ─────────────────────────────
A ─────────────────────────────
B ─────────────────────────────
```

Tablature *(Tabs)*

On the last page, we saw four lines. This is what we call tablature. Tablature is the full word for what are often known as 'tabs'. This is far more commonly used these days. Tablature is sheet music for ukulele and other stringed instruments. It shows us what notes we have to play through numbers on different strings. In ukulele tabs, the G note (the lowest string which is also closest to you) is the bottom string, the C note the next one along and so on.

The first thing that I would like you to do is to play each note openly: G to A.

In tablature, playing each note openly would look like this:

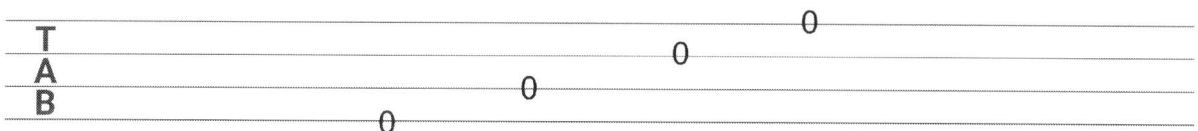

The reason for the 0 is that we aren't actually playing on a fret. The numbers demonstrate which fret we have to put our fingers on. An open string is always marked as a 0 in tablature.

It is time now for our first lesson. In this lesson, we will play a very simple pattern and you will see how it looks when we tab it out.

Lesson:

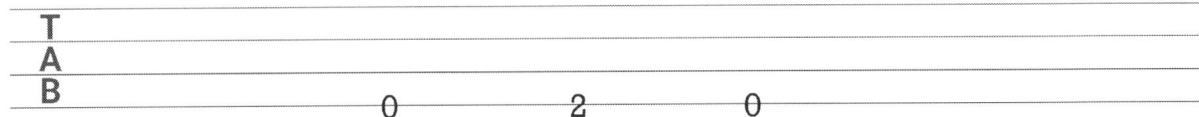

For this lesson, you will be using the G string only.

Step 1: Play the open G string.

Step 2: Place your index finger (or middle finger) on the second fret of the G string and play it. The second fret is the second note away from the nut which is marked by the frets (the lines on the fretboard).

Step 3: Let go and play the G string open again.

We started with a 0 on the G string which marked the fact you played the string open. This was followed by the 2 which means you played the second fret and then we have a 0 again where a string is played openly. Now we are going to include other strings.

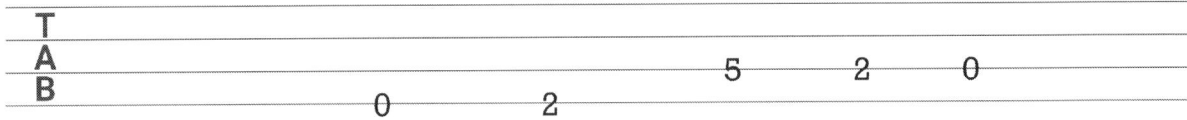

This might look intimidating at first but it really is something you are capable of performing with the knowledge you have acquired so far. Don't worry, I will guide you through.

Step 1: Start the tune by playing the G string open.

Step 2: Just like in the previous exercise, place your finger on the second fret of the G string.

Step 3: Now you want to place your ring finger on the fifth fret of the C string and pluck it.

Step 4: Next, place your index finger on the second fret of the C string.

Step 5: Finish the melody by playing the C string open.

..

The key is to practice this shift over and over until you get the hang of switching between strings. Try switching between other strings as well. We will look at one more exercise in basic tablature before moving forward.

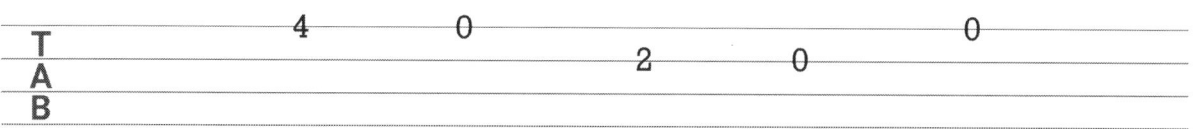

The focus on the previous exercises was on the lower strings. Now we move to the higher strings. This exercise is admittedly more challenging but you can do it. Take it slowly at first and do not rush. Speed comes with time and practice. What is more important is that you play the melody accurately and read the tabs correctly.

Step 1: We start by playing the fourth fret of the A string. Use your ring finger.

Step 2: Then play the A string open.

Step 3: Place your index finger on the second fret of the E string and then play it open.

Step 4: Finish the melody by playing the open A string.

Practice the melody and in your own time, speed up as much as you deem appropriate based on what sounds right to you. It might seem hard at first to group these notes together into a sequence but you'll get there as you improve with repetition.

Separate notes vs grouped notes

Another important element of reading tablature is when you see notes grouped together versus separate. Let's take a look at what this distinction entails.

Look at the two pieces of tablature below. Can you spot the difference?

Diagram (a)

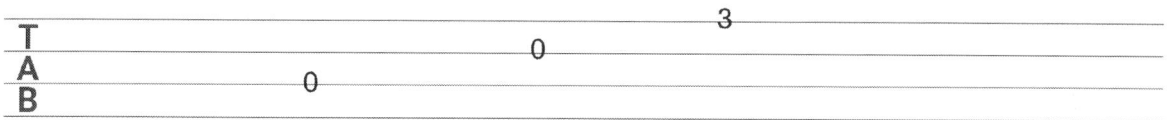

Diagram (b)

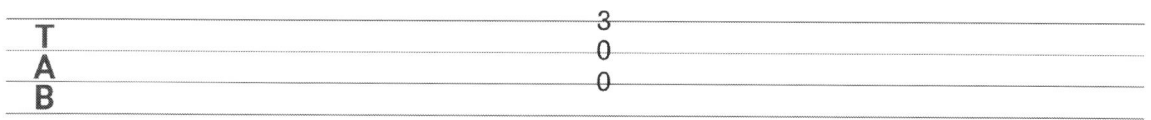

Both diagrams involve the same group of notes: the open C and E strings with the third fret of the A string. However, there is indeed a vital difference between these two diagrams. This is the spacing. When notes are separated as demonstrated in *diagram (a)*, the notes are meant to be played individually and not strummed as a chord. In other words, each note should be picked separately. In this case, you would start by playing the C string, then the E string and finishing on the A string respectively.

In the case of *diagram (b)*, the notes are in line with each other which we call a chord. The notes are meant to be strummed in unison. So instead of playing each note separately, you would have your index or middle finger on the third fret of the A string before playing any note. Then, you would strum the C, E and A strings together. We will come onto chords very shortly but keep in mind the difference between a sequence of notes and grouped notes. One little exercise you can try out is play *diagram (a)* and *(b)* one after the other. Familiarising yourself with the feel of different methods of ukulele playing in the initial stages is the difference between accelerating quickly and learning slower than you could otherwise learn.

. .

One more example to illustrate this point would be as follows:

Diagram (c)

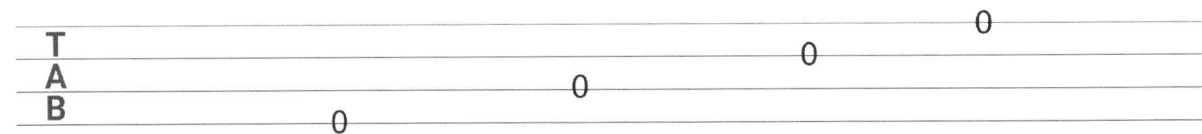

Diagram (d)

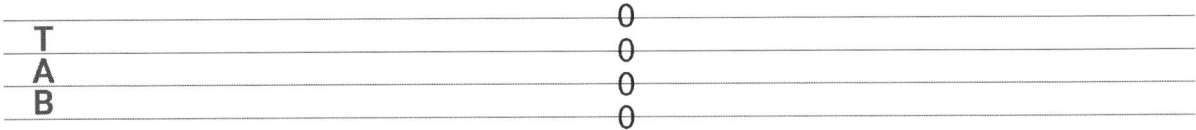

As we observed in the first two diagrams, *diagram (c)* is the individual notation and *diagram (d)* represents the grouped notes. This example is a mile simpler however as it is all open notes. *Diagram (c)* asks of us only to play through each note one by one whereas *diagram (d)* demands us to strum every string together and open. Hopefully this is simple enough.

So what mistakes do people make with tablature. It seems straight forward enough, doesn't it?

Mistake 1: G to A

Well, as simple as it appears to some, reading tablature is a skill and like all skills, you get better at them with the more time and energy you put in. A mistake which you should not make is to **misread** tabs. I once had a student who learned a song in tab form and when he played it back to me, it sounded completely wrong. I asked him if he had learned the correct piece. What had happened is he had learned the right song but was reading the tablature upside down.

As we just learned, tabs are read like this.

```
T
A
B
```

He had made a fatal error, which is surprisingly common, where he saw tabs the wrong way around. So please remember that in tablature, the G string is the string closest to your chest. Not the high string near your knees. Tabs are laid out the way that they are because it is giving you a first hand perspective starting at the G string and going higher up: not lowering down.

Mistake 2: Playing on the fret

This mistake is just a dear as any other and is most prevalent amongst students who haven't been told otherwise or have previous experience playing bass guitar. Cast your mind back to the introductory chapter of this book.

We looked at the fretboard and it's function. The individual frets which are lined on your ukulele neck are the width and size that they are for a reason. Some players make the mistake of playing on the line instead of between the frets. You are meant to play in the middle of the fret, roughly where the dot is and not on the lined fret itself. Many beginners do this and they either end up sounding out of tune or the note is muted and incorrect. Every stringed instrument is different and while with some instruments playing on the fret is good technique, this is not the case with the ukulele. Like other modern stringed instruments, ukuleles are designed to give you maximum comfort and playability.

To clarify, the correct way to play a note:

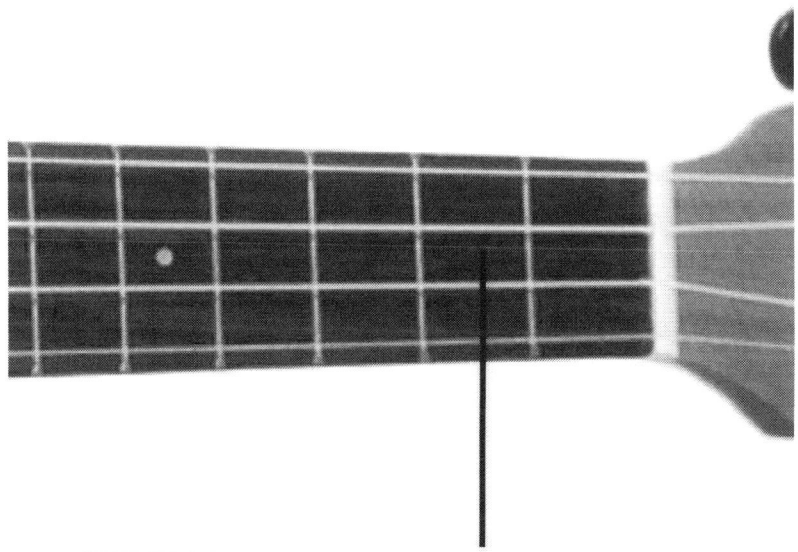

place your finger in the middle of the fret or as near to it as possible.

Day Two: Your First Melodies

Day one is finally complete. Welcome to your second day which promises to be more fun. This was emphasised in the introduction but we do insist that you move on to the following day only when you have mastered the previous day. If you are still uncertain with concerns to tablature and reading ukulele music, revise day one with precision and once you have grasped everything, come back to day two.

With that said, it's time to look at your first melodies. In this chapter, we will be covering three unique melodies of varying difficulty. The first one will be an absolute beginner's tune, the second more intermediate and the third will be in the advanced range of the beginner spectrum. All three are playable though and none should be too difficult for a beginner provided that you practice each one until you have perfected it.

Melody 1:

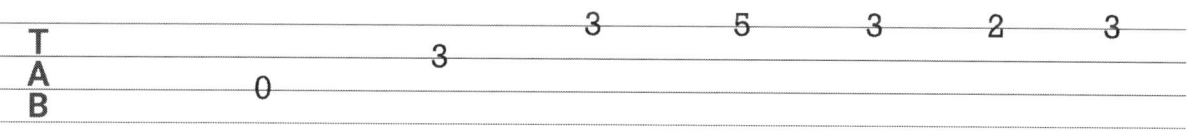

Melody one is a simple jig in the key of C major. Do not be intimidated! We have you covered. Let us break it down for you. Always start out slowly and build up speed once you are more confident.

Step 1: Start by playing the open C string with your right hand.

Step 2: Place your index finger on the third fret of the E string.

Step 3: For easier transition to the higher notes that follow, take your index finger off the third fret of the E string and place it one string up onto the third fret of the A string.

Step 4: Place your ring finger on the fifth fret of the A string.

Step 5: Move back down to the third fret of the A string playing it with the index finger again.

Step 5: Move your index finger down one fret to the second fret of the A string.

Step 6: Finish the melody on the C note which is the third fret of the A string with your index finger.

Please note that if you find using your middle finger easier, then please go ahead but for the average player, the index finger works best as the pointing leading finger when fretting a melody.

Melody 2:

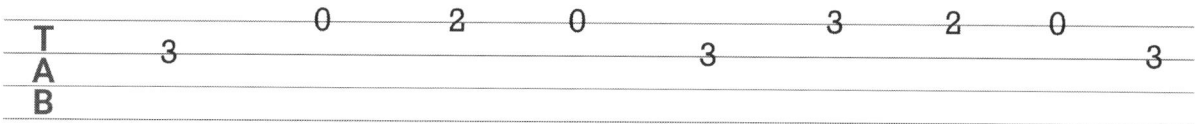

We move onto melody number two. This one is slightly more advanced and involves are more in depth fingering. Make note that this melody is in the key of G major.

Step 1: Begin by playing the third fret of the E string with your **middle finger**. This is important because your index and ring fingers need to be free to navigate the A string later on.

Step 2: Play the open A string.

Step 3: Place your index finger on the second fret of the A string and then once you've played it, take your finger off and play the A string open once more.

Step 4: Return to the third fret of the E string with your middle finger.

Step 5: Now you're going to move your middle finger off the E string and use it on the third fret of the A string - one string up.

Step 6: Use your index finger to play the second fret of the A string and then play it open. Finish the melody with your middle finger on the third fret of the E string.

Melody two certainly entails more dexterity than melody one but practice, practice, practice! You will get there.

Melody 3:

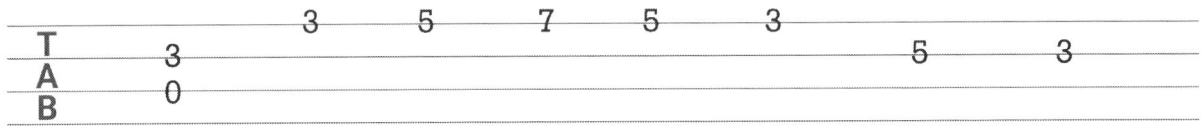

Melody three is once again in the key of C major. For this melody, you will need to cast your mind back to day one where we spoke about separated and unseparated notes. The melody starts with unseparated notes in a micro-chord.

Step 1: Place your index finger on the third fret of the E string and strum it together with the open C string. This takes precision and ensure you do not strum any other strings.

Step 2: We now have a little 'run-down'. Run downs are a series of notes on a string or strings whereby you go up and down in a sequence. In this case, place your index finger on the third fret of the A string. Move up to the fifth fret using your ring finger and then place your pinky on the seventh fret.

Step 3: We now come back down. Using the same fingering going up, we will do the reverse. Play the fifth fret of the A string using your ring finger and then finish with your index finger on the third fret.

Step 4: The melody ends on the E string. Place your ring finger on the fifth fret of the E string and then your index finger on the third fret of the same string.

You will find plenty more melodies in the practice songs in the final chapter of this book. Try perfecting the three we have covered in this chapter. It should be stated that many ukulele players just like guitarists believe that speed is important. It isn't and I would go as far as saying that it is more or less irrelevant when starting out. Ensuring your fingering is on point and that you aren't facing hiccups or false notes are far more essential aspects of ukulele playing. Speed will come with time and practice. Frustration is also inevitable when you are in your first steps of learning an instrument. If you find something is too challenging or you aren't advancing at the rate you had hoped, don't give up and try not to get worked up. We all learn at different rates and the ukulele isn't meant to be an easy instrument. But. you can and will get there! Believe that with all of your courage because the reward is much sweeter when you are able to overcome the hurdles of the beginning.

Day Three: Chords & Progressions

Day three is all about chords. Chords are extremely popular amongst players of all abilities because they enable us to adapt any song to chords we know and so the appeal of strumming your way through a tune is greater than learning the tablature. Chords are groups of notes (typically between *2* and *5* notes) strummed in unison. In this chapter, you will be introduced to basic chord shapes and then you will learn how to play them together to form what are called **chord progressions**.

Chords are a step up from individual tabs since multiple notes are being played in one single strum plus there is the added expense of having to pick correctly and then change shape.

Do not fret! This chapter will help you with all of the potential hurdles and before you know it, you'll be jamming away through songs with ease. Be patient, practice each exercise and take your time. Learning chords on ukulele can be a frustrating process but keep with it. It is worth the hard work that you put in.

We'll be looking at the following chords to start off with :

C major, G major, A minor and F major.

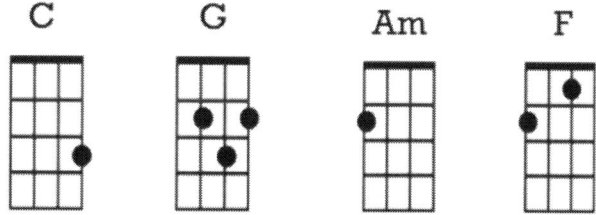

We will begin with the chord that all beginners ought to know like the back of their hand. The ***C major*** chord.

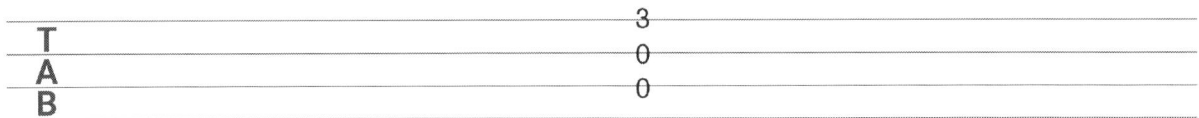

This is what the chord looks like when written out. C major on the ukulele is the simplest chord to play since it only involves one finger being used.

Step 1: To start the chord, place your index finger (pointer) on the third fret of the A string.

Step 2: Strum the C, E and A strings. i.e. the top three strings of the ukulele.

If you got it right, you should hear the beautiful sound of a C chord.

Do not move on to the next chord until you have a good grasp of the C chord. An exercise which you must learn to do is to play a new chord and then remove all your fingers from the instrument. After a few seconds, try to re-find the fingering and play the chord again from memory. This method, employed by top musicians (particularly guitarists) helps your muscle memory increase drastically. It is arduous at first but the more you try it, the better you'll get the hang of it.

Our second chord is the *G major* chord.

```
T ─────────────────2─────────
A ─────────────────3─────────
  ─────────────────2─────────
B ───────────────────────────
```

So right off the bat, I'm going to be completely honest with you: on every stringed instrument whether it be the mandolin, guitar or ukulele, the G chord has a way of somehow being the most frustrating chord to learn. Unfortunately, we have to roll with it and just face it head on. Again, once you learn the fingering for the chord, repeat the shape as hard as it may be. Muscle memory never fails a ukulele player!

Step 1: Place your index finger on the second fret of the C string.

Step 2: Place your ring finger (yes I know it feels weird) on the third fret of the E string.

Step 3: Finish with the middle finger tucked underneath it on the A string.

If you ever saw the 90s sitcom *Friends*, this is the chord shape that Phoebe called the 'bear claw' because your fingers resemble those of a creature with scrunched paws. Or maybe even Yoda from Star Wars…

. .

Exercise

Before moving on to the third chord, it is time for an exercise. We have covered two essential chords and it would benefit you to focus on these before moving on. To really make these chords stick in your memory, you need to put them into practical use. So we are going to practice an exercise whereby you will play the C chord and the G chord in sequence as follows.

C   *G*   *C*   *G*

Take your time with it ! Practice it until it flows naturally and then move on to the next chord shape. It's important to practice every chord as you go along as opposed to cramming them in later. The more you become used to associating a chord name with its shape, the easier you'll find practicing songs later on when you have no visual prompter or tab to help you.

..

Our third chord shape is A minor. This is similar to the C chord in that it involves a singe finger on the fretting hand.

```
T ─────────────────────0─────────
A ─────────────────────0─────────
A ─────────────────────0─────────
B ─────────────────────2─────────
```

Step 1: To play this chord, begin by placing your index finger or middle finger (if you prefer) in the second fret of the G string.

Step 2: That's pretty much it. Now you strum the four strings.

If you are new to music, minor chords are supposed to sound sad and they act really well with major chords (the 'happy' sounding chords). In modern pop music, you typically find one minor chord in a progression of four chords but we will come onto chord progressions in due course.

Exercise

It is time for an exercise again. At this point, having learned three chords: one of which was a pretty challenging one, we need to practice bringing them together and incorporating the A minor with the two major chords.

For this exercise, we are going to play a chord progression. It is simpler than it looks so give it as much of a chance as you can. Play it slowly and take as much time as you need to switch chord shapes.

The progression is:

C   G   Am   C

In this sequence, we are starting out on a C major chord, moving to G, then the A minor (which is arguably the most uphill part of this exercise) and then back to C. It's a challenge because shifting from a three finger chord to a one finger chord can be quite an experience when starting out. This exercise is not random nor pointless though because practicing it and getting a grasp of it will help you with three key aspects of ukulele playing.

1. Switching between chords.
2. Muscle memory and increased finger agility.
3. Returning back to the key note (C) after having played other chords.

Point three is particularly indispensable because in any genre of music, it is one thing to be able to switch chords but what makes a musician particularly skilled is the ability to return to the starting chord/note having gone through the progression. In this case, C major is your anchor. Focus on points 1 and 2 but also put extra practice into going from the G major and A minor back to the C major.

C

```
T|-----------------3-----------|
A|-----------------0-----------|
B|-----------------0-----------|
 |-----------------------------|
```

G

```
T|-----------------2-----------|
A|-----------------3-----------|
B|-----------------2-----------|
 |-----------------------------|
```

Am

```
T|-----------------0-----------|
A|-----------------0-----------|
B|-----------------0-----------|
 |-----------------2-----------|
```

C

```
T|-----------------3-----------|
A|-----------------0-----------|
B|-----------------0-----------|
 |-----------------------------|
```

The next chord we will look at is the F major chord.

This chord can appear to be quite tricky but if you nail this one down, you'll really be making progress in your ukulele journey. The F major chord uses two fingers in what is actually quite a stretch if you're brand new. Don't panic though because you will get there. As repetitive as I have been about it: practice will make you the best uke player you can be.

```
T |---------------|-0-|---------------
A |---------------|-1-|---------------
A |---------------|-0-|---------------
B |---------------|-2-|---------------
```

The F chord is different to the previous chords we have looked at because the leading finger which for a lot of chords is typically the index finger, is actually the middle finger.

Step 1: Start by placing your middle finger on the second fret of the G string.

Step 2: Keeping the G string firmly pressed down, place your index finger on the first fret of the E string. Remember, we are skipping a string so be sure you aren't placing your index finger on the first fret of the C string otherwise you will get an A major chord which is fine but **NOT** what we are going for here.

If you're starting out, do not be disheartened if you find this fingering particularly difficult. You aren't expected to perfect the F major chord when you're just a few days into playing. However, in your own time and without rushing, do try to memorise the shape of the F chord. Another good exercise is performing the shape away from the instrument and just in your day to day life. The muscles in your hand will strengthen and become used to the stretch.

The final chord which we will look at is the D major chord. I wish I had better news for you but this chord is another tough one. Still, you need to be introduced to these chords because while they can be hard, they are essential and the D major chord is one of the most recurring chords in music.

```
T|----------------------------5-----
 |----------------------------2-----
A|----------------------------2-----
B|----------------------------------
```

The D major is a three finger chord.

Step 1: Place your index finger on the second fret of the C string.

Step 2: Place your middle finger just underneath it on the second fret of the E string.

Step 3: Now for the stretch. Place your pinky finger (*yes that's right: pinky finger*) on the fifth fret of the A string. Strum the chord.

You might be aware that the chord looks a bit peculiar. It's probably because you are leaving a two fret gap. Don't worry, it's meant to feel and look like that. Strum the entire chord making sure your index and middle finger are not muting each other. If your fingers are muting these strings a bit, it's because your shape needs to be more accurate.

Accurate fingerings are what make the ukulele sound crisp and professional. If you do find yourself in a situation of buzzing or muting, bend the fingers a little bit and make sure you are pressing hard enough on the string. There will be a little bit of pain if you are new to stringed fretted instruments but your finger tips will callus with time and practice and no longer cause any issues.

We have now covered the basic chords needed when starting out on the ukulele. There are many other chords which you need to learn and they are included on the opening page so please do refer to the diagram and learn some of the other chords at your own volition. I would recommend looking at the A major chord and B minor chord to begin with.

A major

```
T|-------------------0-------------
A|-------------------0-------------
 |-------------------1-------------
B|-------------------2-------------
```

B minor

```
 |-------------------2-------------
T|-------------------2-------------
A|-------------------2-------------
B|-------------------x-------------
```

In the B minor chord, you might be wondering what the X is. In tablature, when you see an X, it signifies that you do not play that string at all.

With what's been covered so far, you should have all the knowledge and skill required to teach yourself some of the other chord shapes so don't be shy or intimidated, you can do it and I believe you will be an awesome ukulele player who is going to be able to play any chord on demand in no time!

Chord Progressions

Chord progressions put the chords you've learned into practice and turn sound into music. We have already looked at a few with the C, G and A minor chords.

To recap, chord progressions are series of chords played in a sequence to complement each other. They are vital to know since when you write your own music or when you are accompanying another ukulele player/guitarist/other musician in general, it is key to know which chords go with other ones.

Here are some more progressions for you to try out. Remember that each chord is worth one strum.

- **C-C-G-G-Am-Am-F-F**
- **C-G-C-G-G-F-C**
- **G-F-Am-G-F-Am-C**
- **D-D-D-D-G-G-G-G-D**
- **F-F-F-F-G-G-G-G-Am-Am-Am-Am-Am-C**
- **D-D-A-A-Bm-Bm-G-G**
- **C-G-F-G-C**
- **D-G-D-G-A-D-G-D**

..

Like with tablature and tuning, we will now focus on the mistakes people make with chords and how to overcome them.

Mistake 1: Sloppiness and Taking 'Easy' Chords For Granted

I will go ahead and make a declarative statement: chords are where most beginners fail. Once more, this is not due to their abilities as musicians but easily avoidable errors. Students will learn their first few chords and then they'll proceed to strum away and think "this is easy". If you do not focus on your positioning and fretting when you're starting out, you run the risk of rushing ahead. This will lead to poor musicianship and technique in the long run. ***What am I talking about?***

Think back to when you learned tabs and melodies in days one and two. You probably noticed that you had to break down each pattern and note to get it right. You should pay the same amount of focus to chords. The C chord looks easy and straight forward. Granted, it is - especially in comparison to some other chord shapes that you will come across in your life as a musician. What I am getting at is : don't assume that just because the chord has one fretted note in it that that it is easy. The C chord is sloppily played by beginners who don't ensure accuracy. Common mistakes of this kind are playing off the fret, on the second fret or simply strumming three out of the four strings which is also wrong. Take the time to strum delicately and fret accurately. In time, your muscle memory will catch on and every chord you play will be smooth and consistently faultless.

Mistake 2: Poor Hand Position

This mistake occurs very frequently and yet is seldom talked about in beginner's guides to ukulele. Sometimes, especially when playing more advanced chords like D major, players find that there is pain in their fingers or that the position is beyond a level of comfort that they can withstand. In lieu of finding a solution, beginners either give up on the chords or find simplified versions of them. While both proposed solutions might sound appealing, they both negate the purpose of learning a new instrument and the hurdles that come with such a task.

Believe it or not, contrary to popular belief, the most likely culprit for why your hand doesn't feel right or is at a high level of discomfort when playing is your hand position. I want you to perform a practical exercise right now. Choose a chord to play and get your hand into that position.

Take a look at your **wrist** and your **palm**. These two areas are pivotal for successful fretboard and neck navigation. The flesh of your palm should never be pressed completely against the neck. At most, it can gently touch it. If your palm does press hard against the neck when you play, this will cause you a great deal of agony when playing. Instead, when fingering a chord, curl your fingers more by bending your knuckles. Don't be static especially in your index and middle fingers. This will act as a pivot. The part of your hand that should be touching the neck is the gap between your thumb and forefinger. This creates a much easier environment for utmost success with ease.

Day Four: Important Techniques

Welcome to day four. Hopefully you will feel as though you have made indispensable progress because in reality: you have. Give yourself a pat on the back. You truly deserve it. I would go as far as saying that in theory, you have all the basic knowledge you need to navigate the ukulele at your own volition. However, a little more guidance is surely needed at this stage. While in the previous days, we covered simplicities and theoretical knowledge, we move forward onto techniques or should I say 'technicalities'. These are designed to help you perfect and improve your playing. A technique in some ways might appear easier than a whole new concept on ukulele but in other ways, techniques are actually harder. Not because they take more skill but because they help a player understand the music they are playing as opposed to just following along with tabs and sheet music. To a large extent, they are the difference between a player who can simply play a few notes and a musician who knows the purpose of those notes.

What is meant by **purpose**?

Sometimes, especially in basic ukulele, you might play a set of notes which make up a melody. However, knowing why you are playing those notes and how they fit in with the song is a whole other thing. Techniques such as the ones we will cover in the following chapters help you understand the music you are playing. In this way, with confidence and practice, you'll be able to make any melody your own.

We start with **pull-offs** and **hammer-ons**.

Both are remarkably common in the world of electric guitar and even bass. Advanced ukulele players use them all of the time too and while they sound like complicated or weird concepts, they really aren't if you learn how to practice them properly and you get the technique right.

1. What is a *hammer-on*?

While the name sounds like something out of nordic war epic, the name actually makes complete sense with what it is. A hammer-on is when you play a note and then play a different note on the same string but instead of picking it you just hit it with a different finger i.e. hammering on. Your finger acts as a 'hammer' of sorts to strike a note without plucking it, using the momentum from the previously strum note.

In ukulele tablature, a hammer-on is identified by this symbol:

‘

Let's take a look at how a hammer-on might look like in a piece of music.

```
            3      '5
T
A
B
```

In this example, we are going from the third fret of the A string to the fifth fret. So what's so unique about this? Simply, instead of picking the fifth fret as an individual note, you don't. Let me break it down for you step by step so you can fully understand how this technique works.

Step 1: Place your index finger on the third fret of the A string. Pluck it or pick it as you normally would.

Step 2: With some force, hit the fifth fret of the A string with your ring finger without plucking or picking it separately. If done right, you would have heard the fifth fret being played without using your right hand. This is a ***hammer-on***.

The function of hammer-ons might seem banal and useless in the context of an exercise but when you use them in songs, they not only improve the quality of your skill-set but they can make a lick or riff sounds very professional.

Before we move on, let's try out an exercise where hammer-ons are used. The exercise is straight forward but make sure to play it slowly at first getting the hang of the fingering. When you're confident enough to do so, speed it up at your own volition.

Exercise:

```
T|---------------------------------3------|
A|-----------------0----------------------|
B|-------0--------------------------------|
```

```
T|----------------3------'5------3--------
A|-----------------------------------------
B|-----------------------------------------
```

To really comprehend what's going on, let's break this riff down.

Step 1: Begin by playing the open C and E strings.

Step 2: Now, place your index finger on the third fret of the A string as you did in the first exercise.

Step 3: Now for the hammer-on. Hit the fifth fret using just your ring finger.

Step 4: Go back to the third fret of the A string with your index finger and pick it normally.

2. What is a *pull-off*?

A pull off is almost the opposite of a hammer-on, but not quite. A pull-off is what it sounds like. It is when you go down a note by 'pulling' off from a note. Instead of removing your finger entirely and playing the next note separately, you will use the finger already on the fret by push it down, letting go and letting the string ring out. Let's use the same example as we did with the hammer-on.

In ukulele tablature, a pull-off is identified by this symbol:

$$//$$

Just like the last example, have look at the diagram below. Let's say you have played the fifth fret of the A string and want to go down to the third fret. Instead of playing it as a lone note (by re-picking the string on the third fret), you want to perform a pull-off to make the sequence smoother.

```
T ─────────────5//──────3──────────
A ─────────────────────────────────
B ─────────────────────────────────
```

Step 1: Place your ring finger on the fifth fret of the A string.

Step 2: While you are playing the fifth fret, have your index finger already on the third fret ready to be played. So now, you should have two fingers on the A string: one on the third fret and one on the fifth.

Step 3: Pick the fifth fret as you normally would.

Step 4: Now quickly, as the note is playing, pull the string downwards with your fretting finger and finally off the string while letting it ring out. This should let the third fret of the A string (the C note) ring out. This is a pull-off as you are literally pulling off from a note onto one lower than it.

Soloing in C

What has been acknowledged in day three is the fact that to most beginners, all things to do with C major are very appealing. It's always the first chord people learn and it is usually the go-to key for beginners who try to learn songs on their own? Why is this? Simply because it is easy. It's a one finger chord using one note on one fret. Plus, many pop songs use C as the basis.

So knowing that C is popular, beautiful sounding and straight forward, we've decided to dedicate a chapter to making your C chord go further. That is, how can you as a debutant on ukulele make the C chord become something more. Specifically, we will look at how notes in the C major scale on the ukulele can help you write easy but cool sounding solos using minimal effort and a solid understanding of the notes in C.

Diagram (a)

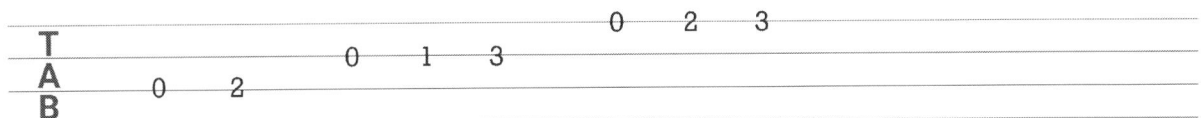

Take a look at the diagram above. This diagram is not a melody but rather a the C major scale. They are all notes which can be formulated (however you please) to make a melody in C. In fact, the traditional song "Amazing Grace" which is in C major uses these notes. You will find the tablature and chords for this classic in the final chapter of this book. In the first instance, I want you to play the scale about and familiarise yourself with the individual notes. The next step once you are up to speed with the C major scale is putting it into practice. We'll start with two basic compositions in C major that we have put together. Then, you will be encouraged to create your own using the notes from the C major scale as demonstrated in diagram (a).

Composition 1:

```
T|-----------------------------5-------------|
A|-------------------3-----------------------|
B|---------0---------------------------------|


T|---------7---------5---------8---------7---|
A|-------------------------------------------|
B|-------------------------------------------|


T|-------------------------------------------|
A|-------------------------------------------|
B|---------2---------0---------0-------------|


T|---------3---------1-----------------------|
A|-----------------------------4---------4---|
B|-------------------------------------------|
```

 :|

Composition 2:

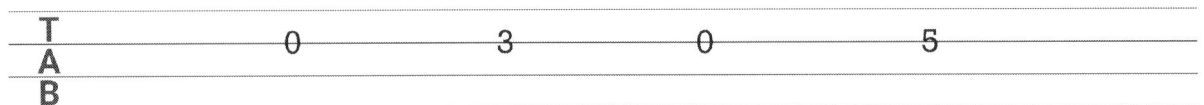

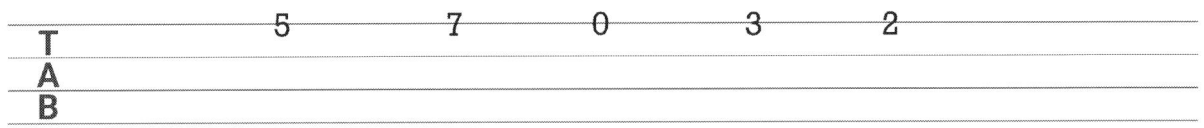

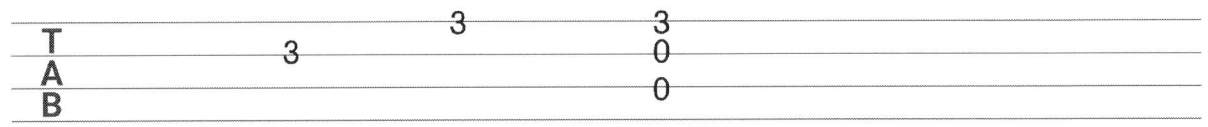

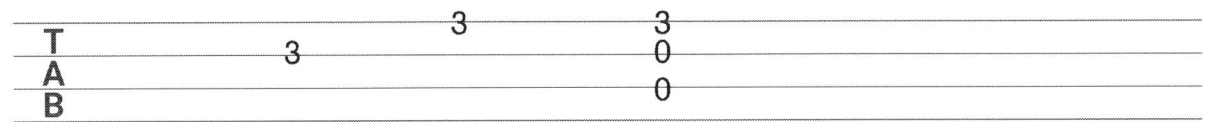

It is now your turn to write out a composition in C using the C major scale and the examples in the previous two compositions.

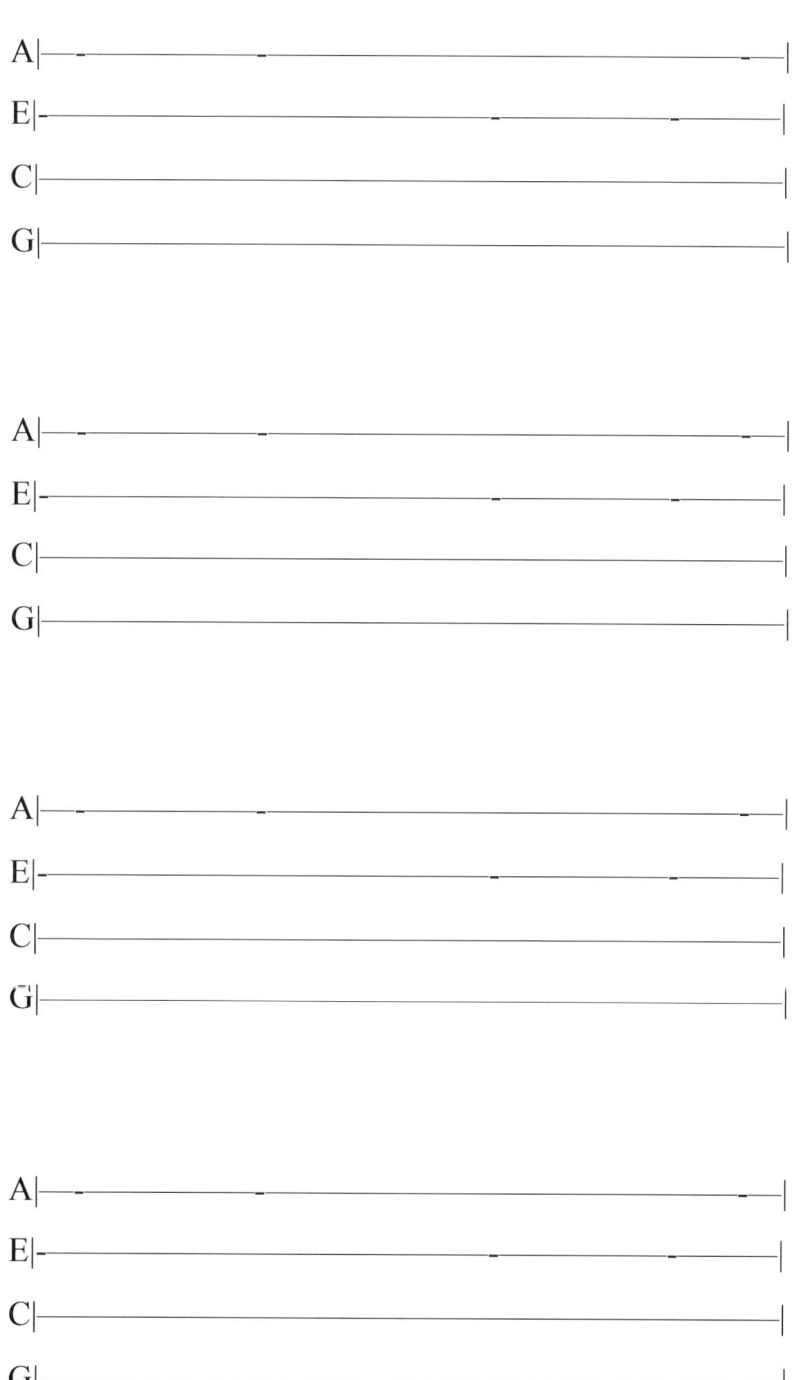

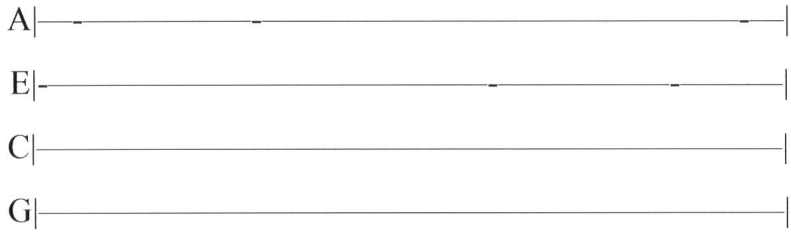

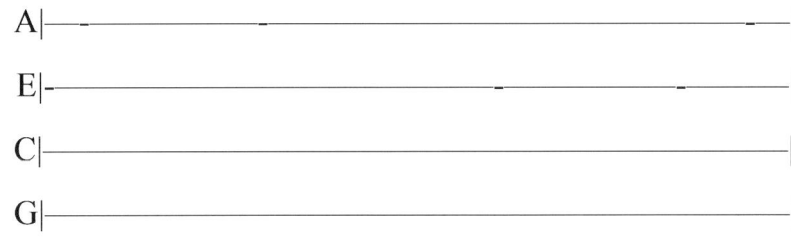

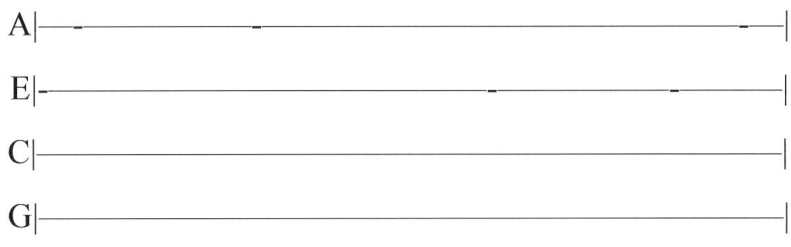

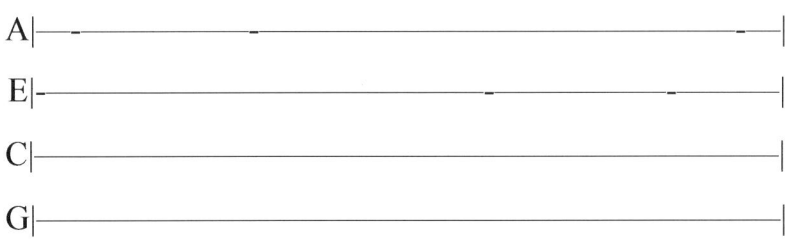

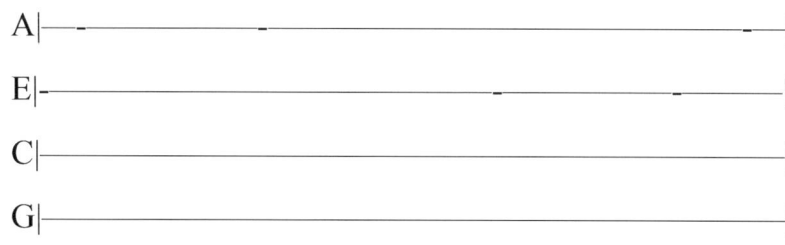

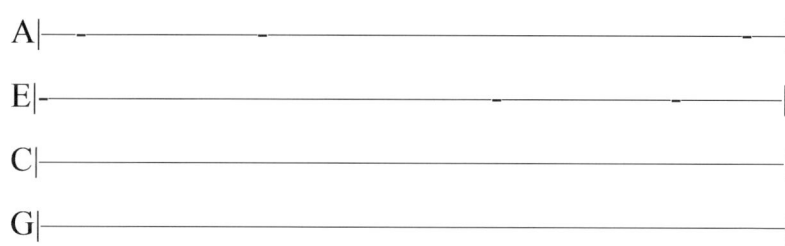

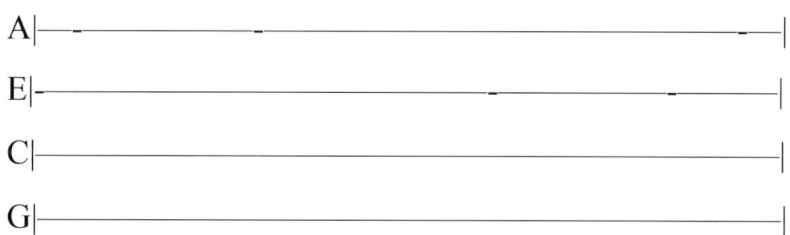

Barring

In this segment, you will be introduced to the concept of barring. This is for all intent and purposes a more advanced technique. If you have had any experience playing the guitar, at some point you would have come across barre chords. Whenever students are taught them for the first time, there is always an unanimous moan because barre chords by nature are not easy for the budding beginner. Well, there's more bad news for you: if you're learning the ukulele to get away from such a technique, you're in for a long night because lo and behold, barre chords exist on ukulele too!

If you have not played guitar before, don't worry. Everything will be explained in this chapter. Let's get into what barre chords are.

I want you cast your mind back to when we learned the D major chord.

It looks like this:

```
T |--------------5--------|
A |--------------2--------|
  |--------------2--------|
B |--------------2--------|
```

At least, that's the way you were taught in the introduction to chords. Now that you've become more acquainted with your instrument, it's time for me to drop a bomb shell: there is a more professional and detailed version of a D chord.

It looks like this:

```
T|-------------------5-----
 |-------------------2-----
A|-------------------2-----
B|-------------------2-----
```

The big deal is : how are you supposed to play the G string on the second fret when your index finger, middle finger and ring finger are all occupied? You might say that we can use our pinky and adjust our hand but this is illogical and would make playing the chord exceedingly uncomfortable for our fingers.

So we do what is called *barring*.

Barring means that instead of using multiple fingers on the same fret (in this case, the second fret), we use one finger (usually our index finger) to cover multiple strings on the same fret. Therefore, we would barre the second fret with our index finger. How is this done, you might ask? Let's take it step by step, as always.

Step 1: Take your index finger and press it hard against the second fret covering all the strings. It will look a bit strange but it's meant to. Ensure your finger is covering every string and is firmly pressing down the fret. This is the trickiest step and it's common to not press hard enough. Don't give up if it seems hard at first.

Step 2: Use your pinky to play the fifth fret of the A string.

Step 3: Strum the chord. If this is your first time barring, it is not unusual for some of the strings to sound muted or blocked. In this instance, press harder with your index finger. I'm afraid there is no easier way around this and it's something you need to persevere with until it clicks. Try not to get frustrated and please ensure you don't injure yourself in the process. It's always better to walk away from a technique for a while before returning to it later than causing yourself grief in the moment.

The shape of the barre chord which we have looked at can be used **anywhere** on the fretboard. Let's look at an E major chord which uses the same barring but instead of starting on the second fret, we have our root on the fourth fret.

```
T ─────────────7─────────────
A ─────────────4─────────────
B ─────────────4─────────────
              4
```

Fifth & Seventh Chords

Fifth and seventh chords are used a lot in jazz music. On ukulele, you can incorporate them in just about any style of playing and they sound absolutely delightful. We start with seventh chords.

What are *seventh chords*?

A seventh chord is a regular chord with one key difference: it contains a note which is seven notes above the root note. So if we are playing an F major chord, we would include an E note because E is seven notes above the F.

F G A B C D E

Normally, the F major chord would contain:

F A C

```
T|------------------0------------------|
A|------------------1------------------|
 |------------------0------------------|
B|------------------2------------------|
```

In the diagram on the previous page, the second fret of the G string is an A note, the open C string is inevitably a C note, the first fret of the E string produces an F note and the open A string is also an A note. So a regular F major chord on the ukulele is composed of an F note, 2 A notes, and a C note. Simply put: F, A, and C.

So how do we transform it into a seventh? As aforementioned, we add an E note.

```
T |----------------0---------
A |----------------1---------
  |----------------3---------
B |----------------2---------
```

This is what it looks like. To achieve the F7 chord (the name of the F major chord when the seventh note is added):

Step 1: Place your middle finger on the second fret of the G string.

Step 2: Then, place your ring finger on the third fret of the C string. **This is the E note.**

Step 3: Finally, place your index finger on the first fret of the E string and strum the entire chord.

The best part of playing seventh chords is that you can incorporate them in any song. You can even turn regular songs into more jazzy sounding versions by adding one or two of them into your playing. Note that not every chord you play in a jazz song needs to be a seventh. Even one can change the dynamic. Try this chord pattern:

C G Am F7

We encountered C, G, and A minor in the previous chapter so if you need to familiarise yourself with these, go back for a recap if need be.

Let's look at another seventh chord. This one is the C major 7 or C7. Just like with the F7, we take the seventh note from the C and add it into our chord shape.

The seventh note of a C major is B.

<u>C</u> D E F G A <u>B</u>

Normally our beloved *C major chord* looks like this:

```
T|--------------------3--------
A|--------------------0--------
B|--------------------0--------
```

It consists of G E and C. Luckily, on ukulele, adding a B note to the C chord is very easy.

Notice how there are two C notes in our C major chord: one on the third fret of the A string and one which is the open C string.

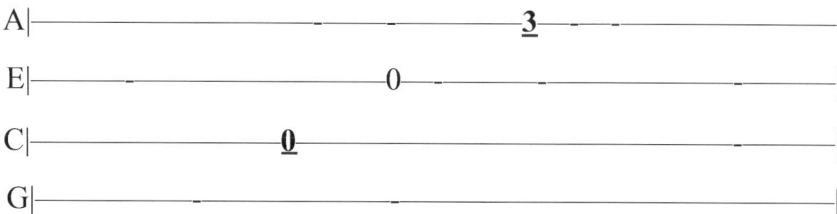

Since we already have a C note on the open C string, all we have to do is turn our C note on the A string into a B note. This is the second fret of the A string.

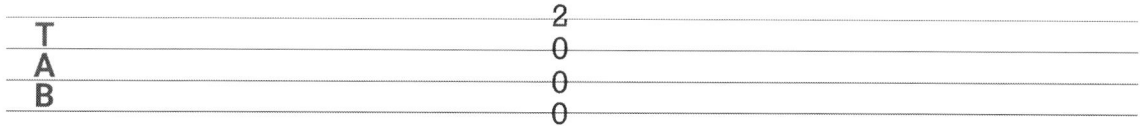

This now makes a **CMajor7** chord because we now have a G, C, E and **B** note.

We have now had a look at two jazz chords. Let's put them together in a pattern:

C7 F7 G

Do not be intimidated by this chord progression. You have seen all of the above chords before. Putting them together takes practice but you will soon realise that it is much simpler than it appears.

We have covered the C7 and the F7 in this chapter. In the previous chapter, we looked at G major. Take your time and do not rush but at the same time, try to play them in the above order.

Before moving on to our second jazz technique, we will look at one final seventh chord. The G major 7 or G7 chord.

As with the C7 and F7, we first have to work out what the seventh note of the G major 7 is.

G A B C D E F

It is the F note. Regularly, a G major chord contains a G, D and E:

```
T|-----------------2---
A|-----------------3---
B|-----------------2---
 |-----------------0---
```

When adding the seventh, this becomes G, D, E and F forming the G7 chord. One which is used often in jazz music.

```
T|-----------------2-----------
A|-----------------1-----------
 |-----------------2-----------
B|-----------------0-----------
```

Step 1: In order to achieve this chord, we start with the same form as the G major by playing the open G string and placing your middle finger on the second fret of the C string.

Step 2: Place your index (pointer) finger on the first fret of the E string. **This is the F note.**

Step 3: Finish by placing your ring finger on the second fret of the A string.

We have now covered the basics of the seventh chord and how you can achieve a magical jazz sound by simply rectifying basic chords by adding a seventh note. You can turn any chord into a seventh by simply adding that note into the equation. For guidance, here are the seventh notes you need for each chord you might play.

A: **A** B C D E F**G**

B: **B** C D E F G**A**

C: **C** D E F G A**B**

D: **D** E F G A B**C**

E: **E** F G A B C**D**

F: **F** G A B C D**E**

G: **G** A B C D E**F**

What is a *fifth chord*?

Fifth chords are also jazz chords. They give a warmer vibe than seventh chords and in this way, they complement seventh chords perfectly. Once you learn about fifth chords, you can mix and max them with seventh chords to create a beautiful jazz medley.

In the next lesson, we will focus specifically on how to form jazz chord progressions and how to put these chords together.

Much like the seventh chords, fifth chords work on the principle of numeracy. To find a fifth chord, you take the root note and count five notes above it. For the first example, we will be looking at an F5 chord, also known as the F major fifth chord.

As we learned in the previous lesson, the seventh of F is E.

<u>F</u> G A B C D <u>E</u>

The fifth on the other hand is C.

<u>F</u> G A B <u>C</u>

So in order to play the F5 chord, we need to add a C. Now you might be confused and say that F **already has** a C in it: **F A C** make up an F major chord.

<u>However, this is where 5th chords are different to seventh chords.</u>

While with seventh chords, the seventh note is added, in fifth chords, particularly in jazz, a fifth note takes priority over the root note and replaces it completely.

What does that mean? It means, you add the fifth note which in this case is C and we remove the F note entirely. In essence, the new note replaces the original note. So in the case of F5, we keep the A and C but use the extra C which is the fifth to take over the F note. It is still an F based chord but the F is what we call *'assumed'*.

In jazz music, assumed notes are not played but implied through the makeup of the other notes.

However, on ukulele, because we are limited to four strings, we do not eliminate the note completely as we normally would, but rather, we emphasise the fifth to almost silence the root note.

So an F5 looks like this.

```
T ─────────────────3─────────
─────────────────1─────────
A ─────────────────0─────────
B ─────────────────2─────────
```

In simple tab form:

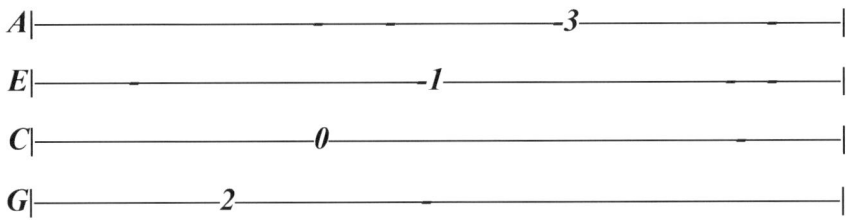

Let's break it down. We begin with the second fret of the G string which is the A note. Then we have the open C string. Next, we play the first fret of the E string and finally we end on that fifth note which takes priority. This is C and is played on the third fret of the A string.

Step 1: Place your middle finger on the second fret of the G string.

Step 2: Place your index finger on the first fret of the E string.

Step 3: Finish the chord by placing your ring finger on the third fret of the A string.

Strum the chord and listen to the beautiful warm jazz chord that has been created. At this point, give yourself a pat on the back as fifth chords are not easy and can be quite challenging to understand.

Now we'll take a look at a C5 chord. This is a welcome chord at this point because it is by far the simplest fifth chord that you will come across when playing jazz ukulele.

The fifth of C is G.

<u>C</u> D E F <u>G</u>

To play the C5 chord, our emphasis will be on the G note.

```
T|-----------------3-----
A|-----------------3-----
A|-----------------0-----
B|-----------------0-----
```

Step 1: Play the open G string and open C strings.

Step 2: Place your index finger on the third fret of the E string. This is our fifth (G note).

Step 3: Place your middle finger on the third fret of the A string.

Strum the chord.

It is worth noting that you can use whatever fingers you feel most comfortable using. The above is simply a recommendation.

The last fifth chord which we will explore is the G5, also known as the G major fifth chord.

The fifth of the G is D.

<u>G</u> A B C <u>D</u>

```
T ―――――――――――――5―――
A ―――――――――――――3―――
  ―――――――――――――2―――
B ―――――――――――――0―――
```

The G5 chord closely resembles the G major chord which we learned earlier in the book. The prime difference is that instead of playing the second fret of the A string which would be a **B** note, we play the fifth fret which is the D note. This completes our fifth chord.

To play the G5:

Step 1: Place your index finger on the second fret of the C string.

Step 2: Place your middle finger on the third fret of the E string. This might feel odd at first because you are essentially tucking your middle finger underneath your index finger but it'll become more natural as you practice the chord shape more regularly.

Step 3: Use your pinky to play the fifth fret of the A string. You can in theory use your ring finger but this will stretch the muscles in that finger in an uncomfortable manner.

Day Five: Strumming & Picking

Day five is here. When first starting out on the ukulele or any stringed instrument for that matter, it is tempting to just strum downwards. However, the earlier you learn how to strum properly, the quicker you'll pick it up. Ukulele players determine how to strum their instrument based on strumming patterns. That is, when the strum downwards and upwards in different amounts. For example, a typical strum is:

down   down   up

(D D U)

This means that the player, with their right hand, will strum down twice and back up once. Strumming down means starting at the bottom string (G) and moving down while hitting all four strings and letting them ring out at once. Strumming upwards involves starting with the high string (A) and doing the same thing as down-strumming but in reverse. Songs rarely start with an up-strum and typically begin with a down-strum. You can practice strumming slowly and build it up to a normal speed. This is an effective way to practice. Don't feel discouraged if you don't get it at first.

It does take time to perfect it and soon, you'll be able to strum to all sorts of strumming patterns. Here are three common strumming patterns that you will come across.

(I recommend that you start practicing these patterns on one chord first before playing multiple chords. Once you feel you've got the hang of it, try two chords and then three or four. After, you may apply strumming patterns to the previous exercises).

D. D. U. D. U. D

(x4)

D. U. D. U. D. U. D. U

(x4)

D. U. D. D. U

(x4)

As with every other day, day five's focus comes with common mistakes. As a matter of fact, an entire book could be written on the subject of strumming and picking. It ought to be strongly noted that there is a massive difference between **strumming** and **picking** and the two are not interchangeable. Strumming is where multiple notes are played together in unison. It is the down or upward motion of striking two or more strings. Picking on the other hand is where you play individual notes separately and each note is distinctive.

Common Mistake: Using Picks

Let's get one thing cleared up: a ukulele is not a guitar. It is far more delicate as we looked at in the introductory index on pages 5 & 6. Therefore, do not assume as a beginner that because it looks like a guitar and is fretted in a similar way that you can use picks like you would on a guitar. This is for two reasons:

1. *The Strings*
2. *Tonality*

The ukulele was designed uniquely to be strum with your hand. The strings on the ukulele (with very few contemporary exceptions) are usually nylon and therefore are basically waiting to break if you go anywhere near them with a typical guitar pick. The only exception to this rule is if you seek out a specific type of pick which is called a ***uke pick***. These are flimsy picks soft enough to be used on the ukulele. In all honesty, unless you have to, I'd stick with using your hands in a lighter more user-friendly approach. With regards to the tonality of the instrument, it's no secret that how you pluck, pick or strum is going to affect the overall output of your ukulele. When using a pick, even of the ukulele variety, you tend to get a gritty, forced sound. That's not what the ukulele was designed to do. Ukuleles are supposed to be beautiful and melodic and so getting a natural feel for them using your fingers will subsequently lead to the sought-after sound which we all know and love.

PRACTICE SONGS

The Star Spangled Banner
(The USA National Anthem)

Chords Used:

G   C   F

```
G   C        C
Oh say can you see,

                  G
by the dawn's early light,

          C     G       C          C
what so proudly we'd hailed, at the twilight's last gleaming?

G    C
Who's broad stripes and bright stars,

          G   C
through the perilous fight,

           C       G        C
O're the ramparts we'd watched were so gallantly streaming?

                G                   F
And the rockets red glare, the bombs bursting in air,

     C         G
gave proof through the night,

        C
that our flag was still there.

G C       F     G
O say does that star spangled banner yet wave

        C    G C
o're the land of the free___,

         F   G C
and the home of the brave?
```

- -

Twinkle Twinkle, Little Star

Chords Used:

C F G

(Intro)

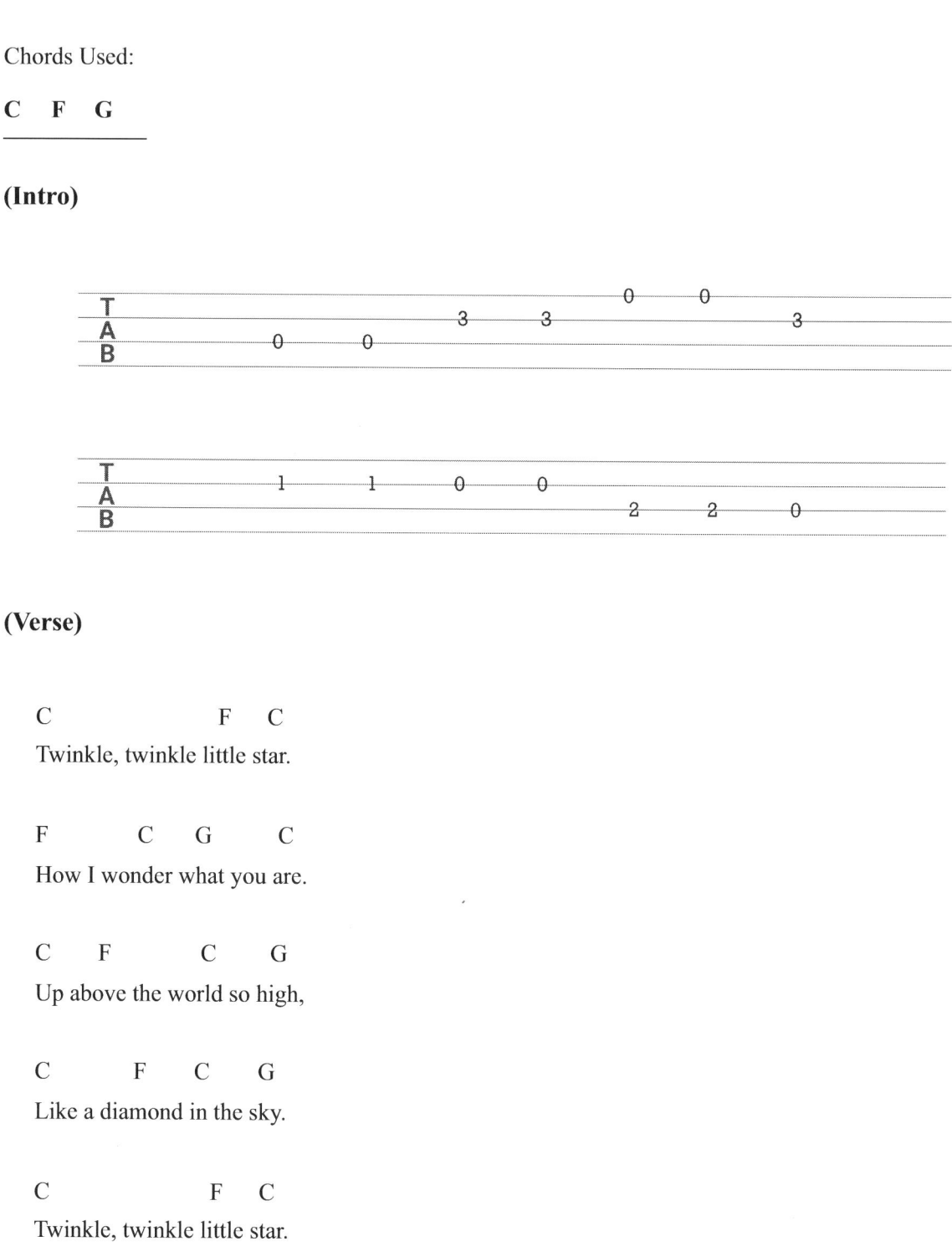

(Verse)

```
C            F  C
```
Twinkle, twinkle little star.

```
F     C   G   C
```
How I wonder what you are.

```
C  F    C   G
```
Up above the world so high,

```
C    F    C   G
```
Like a diamond in the sky.

```
C            F  C
```
Twinkle, twinkle little star.

| F | C | G | C |

How I wonder what you are.

(Verse)

| C | | F | C |

When the blazing sun is gone,

| F | C | G | C |

When she nothing shines upon,

| C | F | C | G |

Then you show your little light,

| C | | F | C |

Twinkle, twinkle, all the night.

| C | | F | C |

Twinkle, twinkle little star.

| F | C | G | C |

How I wonder what you are.

(Verse)

| C | | F | C |

Then the traveler in the dark,

| F | C | | G | C |

Thanks you for your tiny spark,

| C | | F | C | G |

He could not see which way to go,

| C | F | C | G |

If you did not twinkle so.

| C | F | C |

Twinkle, twinkle little star.

| F | C | G | C |

How I wonder what you are.

- -

(Oh) Danny Boy

Chords Used:

C   F   Am   G   Dm

(Intro)

```
T|--------------------------------0---|
A|----------------3---------------|
B|--0-----4-----------------------|

T|------3-----0-------------------|
A|----------------3-----0---------|
B|--------------------------------|

T|--------------------------------|
A|--------------------------------|
B|----------0-----0---------------|
```

(Verse)

```
 C              C            F
Oh Danny Boy, the pipes the pipes are calling

           C     Am    Dm    G
From glen to glen and down the mountain side

           C   C         F
The summer's gone and all the leaves are falling

          C   F   G   C
'Tis you 'tis you must go and I must bide
```

```
    G           C         F     G     C Am  F
    But come you back when summer's in the meadow

    G         Am     F       C    Dm   G
    Or when the valley's hushed and white with snow

              C     Am   F   C Am  F
    'Tis I'll be here in sunshine or in shadow

              C     Am   Dm   G      C
    Oh Danny Boy, oh Danny Boy I love you so
```

(Verse)

```
              C      C         F
    And when you come, and all the leaves are dying

              C    Am   Dm   G  G
    And I am dead, as dead I well may be

              C      C         F
    You'll come and find the place where I am lying

              C    F    G     C
    And stand and say an Ave there for me

    G       C       F    G    C  Am  F
    And I  will hear, though soft you tread above me

    G       Am     F      C   Dm  G
    And in my grave will warmer, safer be

              C     Am   F    C  Am  F
    For you will kneel and tell me that you love me
```

```
         C    Am  Dm    G     C
And I will lie in peace until you come to me
```

- -

America The Beautiful

Chords Used:

C D F G

(Verse)

```
     C         G
O beautiful for spacious skies,

     G         C
for amber waves of grain

               G
For purple mountain majesties,

 D     D    G
above the fruited plain!

  C    G
America! America!

     G         C
God shed his grace on thee

     F         C
And crown thy good with brotherhood,

     F   G   C
from sea to shining sea!
```

(Verse)

   C   G
O beautiful for pilgrim feet,

        G   C
whose stern impassioned stress

               G
A thoroughfare of freedom beat,

D   D G G
across the wilderness!

 C   G
America! America!

    G   C
God mend thine every flaw

  F   C
Confirm thy soul in self-control,

    F G C
Thy liberty in law!

(Verse)

   C   G
O beautiful for heroes proved,

  G   C
in liberating strife.

                G
Who more than self their country loved,

      D   D   G G
and mercy more than life!

 C   G
America! America!

     G   C
May God thy gold refine

   F   C
Till all success be nobleness,

   F   G C
and every gain divine!

(Verse)

    C   G
O beautiful for patriot dream,

    G   C
that sees beyond the years

          G
Thine alabaster cities gleam,

 D   D G
undimmed by human tears!

 C   G
America! America!

     G   C
God shed his grace on thee

     F   C
And crown thy good with brotherhood,

     F   G   C
from sea to shining sea!

- -

Joy To The World

Chords Used:

C   D   G

(Intro)

```
T|------------3-----2-----0-----------
A|------------------------------2-----
B|------------------------------------
```

```
T|------------3-----2-----0-----------
A|------------------------------3-----
B|------------------------------------
```

(Verse)

G   D   G
Joy to the world, the Lord is come!

        C   D   G
Let earth receive her King;

        G   G   G
Let every heart prepare Him room,

         G   G
And Heaven and nature sing,

      D   D
And Heaven and nature sing,

      G   C   G D G
And Heaven, and Heaven, and nature sing.

(Verse)

G   D G
Joy to the earth, the Saviour reigns!

     C   D   G
Let men their songs employ;

        G   G   G
While fields and floods, rocks, hills and plains

 G   G
Repeat the sounding joy,

D   D
Repeat the sounding joy,

 G   C   G D G
Repeat, repeat, the sounding joy.

(Verse)

G   D G
He rules the world with truth and grace,

      C   D   G
And makes the nations prove

    G   G   G
The glories of His righteousness,

    G   G
And wonders of His love,

   D   D
And wonders of His love,

    G   C   G D   G
And wonders, wonders, of His love.

(Verse)

G   D   G
Joy to the world, the Lord is come!

  C   D   G
Let earth receive her King;

  G   G   G
Let every heart prepare Him room,

  G   G
And Heaven and nature sing,

      D   D
And Heaven and nature sing,

      G   C   G D   G
And Heaven, and Heaven, and nature sing.

(Verse)

G   D   G
He rules the world with truth and grace,

     C   D   G
And makes the nations prove

 G   G   G
The glories of His righteousness,

G   G
And wonders of His love,

 D   D
And wonders of His love,

 G   C   G D   G
And wonders, wonders, of His love.

(Outro)

```
T|-----------3----5----3----2----0----2-----
A|-------------------------------------3-----
B|-------------------------------------2-----
```

Michael, Row de Boat Ashore

Chords Used:

C Dm Em F G

(Intro)

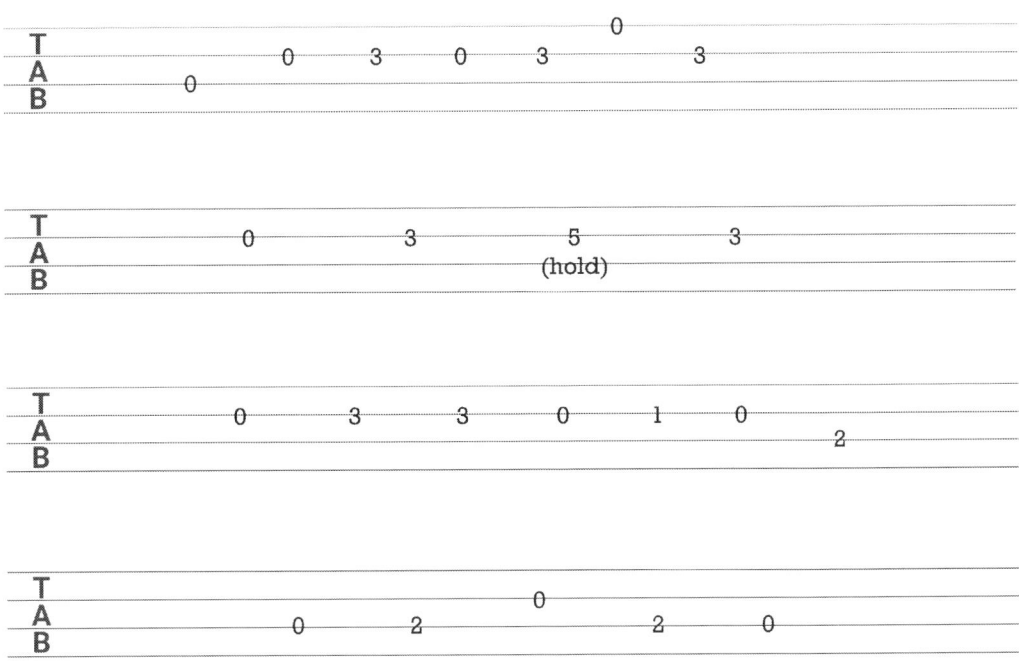

(Chorus)

```
        C              F  C
Michael row the boat ashore, allelu-ya

        Em       Dm    C G   C
Michael row the boat ashore, allelu——ya
```

```
         C                F  C
Sister help to trim the sail, allelu-ya

         Em        Dm     C G   C
Sister help to trim the sail, allelu----ya
```

(Verse)

```
           C                 F    C
Michael's boat is a gospel boat, allelu-ya

         Em          Dm     C G    C
Michael's boat is a gospel boat, allelu——ya

             C                   F     C
The river is deep and the river is wide, allelu-ya

          Em            Dm     C G C
Green pastures on the other side, allelu----ya
```

(Chorus)

```
            C                F   C
Michael row the boat ashore, allelu-ya

          Em        Dm     C G     C
Michael row the boat ashore, allelu——ya

           C                F  C
Sister help to trim the sail, allelu-ya

          Em        Dm     C G  C
Sister help to trim the sail, allelu----ya
```

(Verse)

    C   F C
Jordan's river is chilly and cold, allelu-ya

    Em   Dm C G C
Chills the body but not the soul, allelu——ya

    C   F C
Jordan's river is deep and wide, allelu-ya

    Em   Dm C G C
Meet my mother on the other side, allelu----ya

(Chorus)

    C   F C
Michael row the boat ashore, allelu-ya

    Em   Dm C G C
Michael row the boat ashore, allelu——ya

    C   F C
Sister help to trim the sail, allelu-ya

    Em   Dm C G C
Sister help to trim the sail, allelu——ya.

    C
Hallelu——jah!

    C
Hallelu——jah!

(Outro)

```
T|----------------------------------------|
A|-------------------0--------------------|
A|----0------2---------------2-----0------|
B|----------------------------------------|
```

Jingle Bells

Chords Used:

C Am G A D

(Intro)

```
T|------------2----0---------------5------5------5---|
A|------------------------3--------------------------|
B|-----2---------------------------------------------|
```

```
T|-----5----5----7----5----3----0--------------------|
A|----------------------------------------3----------|
B|---------------------------------------------------|
```

(Verse)

G
Dashing through the snow, in a one-

            C
horse open sleigh,

Am   D
O'er the fields we go, laughing all the

G
way.

   G
Bells on bob-tails ring, making spirits

C
bright,

   Am
What fun it is to ride and sing a

D   G
sleighing song tonight. Oh!

(Chorus)

G   G   C
Jingle bells, jingle bells, Jingle all the

G
way!

 C   G
O what fun it is to ride

       G   A   D
In a one-horse open sleigh, hey!

G   C
Jingle bells, jingle bells, Jingle all the

G
way!

 C   G
O what fun it is to ride

     D   G
In a one-horse open sleigh

(Verse)

  G
A day or two ago, I thought I'd take a

C
ride

  Am
And soon Miss Fanny Bright was

D
seated by my

G
side

                        C
The horse was lean and lank,

Misfortune seemed his lot

  Am   D   D   G   D
We ran into a drifted bank and there we

got

up-sot. Oh!

(Chorus)

G   C
Jingle bells, jingle bells, Jingle all the

G
way!

 C   G

O what fun it is to ride

      A   D

In a one-horse open sleigh, hey!

G   C

Jingle bells, jingle bells, Jingle all the

G
way!

 C   G

O what fun it is to ride

 D   G

In a one-horse open sleigh

(Verse)

  G   C

A day or two ago, the story I must tell

 Am   D

I went out on the snow and on my back

G

I fell

             G
A gent was riding by in a one-horse

      C
open sleigh

  Am   D
He laughed at me as I there lay but

D
quickly drove

G
away. Oh!

[Chorus]

G   C
Jingle bells, jingle bells, Jingle all the

G
way!

 C   G
O what fun it is to ride

   A   D
In a one-horse open sleigh, hey!

G   C
Jingle bells, jingle bells, Jingle all the

G
way!

C   G
O what fun it is to ride

 D   G
In a one-horse open sleigh

[Verse]

G
Now the ground is white, go it while

         C
you're young

 Am   D
Take the girls along and sing this

            G
sleighing song

G
Just bet a bobtailed bay, Two forty as

     C
his speed

 Am   D
Hitch him to an open sleigh and crack!

C
You'll take

G

the lead. Oh!

(Outro)

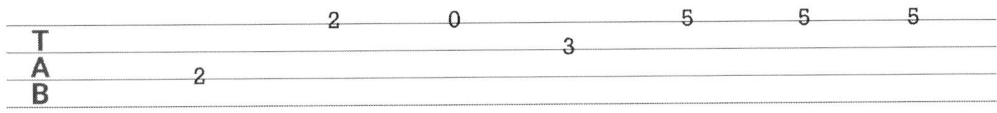

```
T|----------------2----0---------5----5----5-----
A|------2-------------------3---------------------
B|------------------------------------------------

T|------5----5----7----5----3----0---------------
A|----------------------------------3------------
B|------------------------------------------------
```

- -

Hana

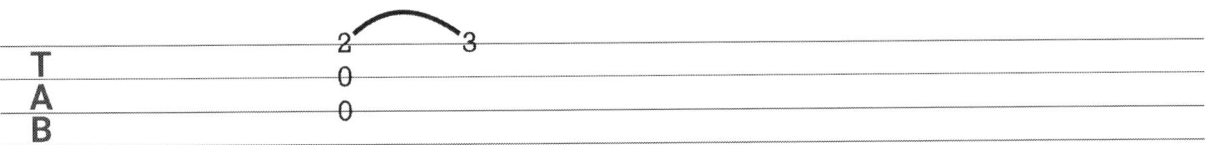
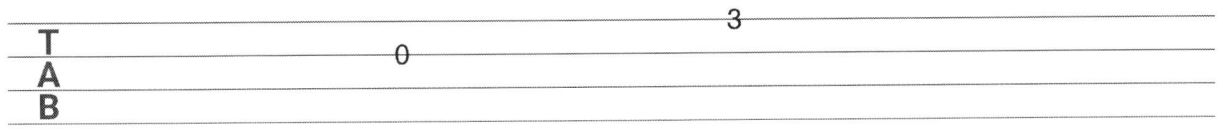
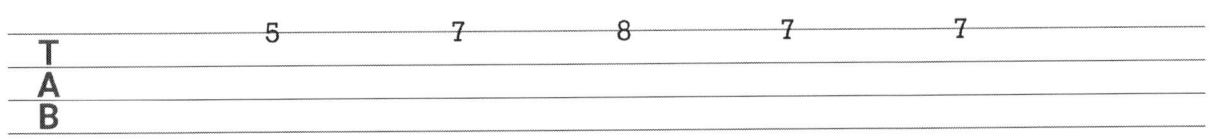
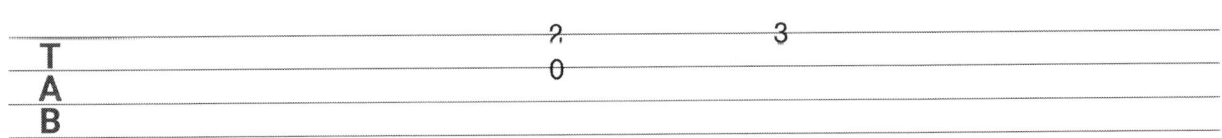
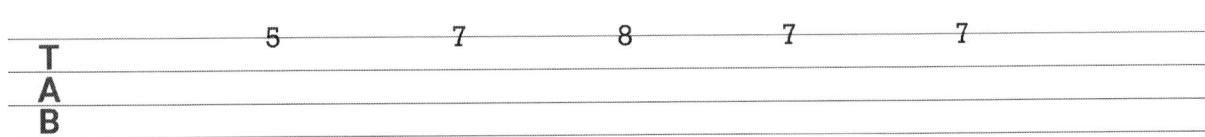

```
T|--------------3-----3-----3-----5-----------|
A|--------0-----------------------------------|
B|--------------------------------------------|


T|---------3-----5-----7-----3----------------|
A|--------------------------------------------|
B|--------------------------------------------|


T|--------5-----7-----5-----3-----------------|
A|--------------------------------------------|
B|--------------------------------------------|


T|--------2-----2-----3-----3-----------------|
A|--------------------------------------------|
B|--------------------------------------------|


T|--------10----------10----12----------------|
A|--------0-----------------------------------|
B|--------0-----------------------------------|
```

```
E|----------------15--------15--------15--------10----------|
B|----------------------------------------------------------|
G|----------------------------------------------------------|
D|----------------------------------------------------------|
A|----------------------------------------------------------|
E|----------------------------------------------------------|


E|----------------12--------15--------12--------------------|
B|----------------------------------------------------------|
G|----------------------------------------------------------|
D|----------------------------------------------------------|
A|----------------------------------------------------------|
E|----------------------------------------------------------|


E|------------------------10--------7-----------------------|
B|----------------------------------------------------------|
G|----------------------------------------------------------|
D|----------------------------------------------------------|
A|----------------------------------------------------------|
E|----------------------------------------------------------|


E|----------------7---------10--------10--------------------|
B|----------------------------------------------------------|
G|----------------------------------------------------------|
D|----------------------------------------------------------|
A|----------------------------------------------------------|
E|----------------------------------------------------------|


E|----------------7----7----8----7----5---------------------|
B|----------------------------------------------------------|
G|----------------------------------------------------------|
D|----------------------------------------------------------|
A|----------------------------------------------------------|
E|----------------------------------------------------------|
```

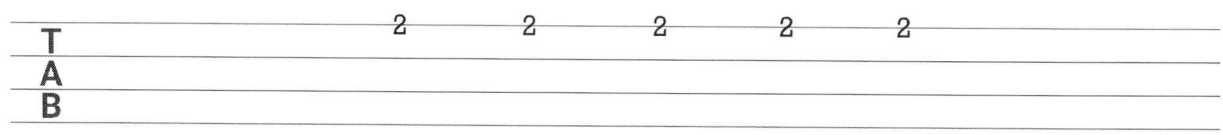

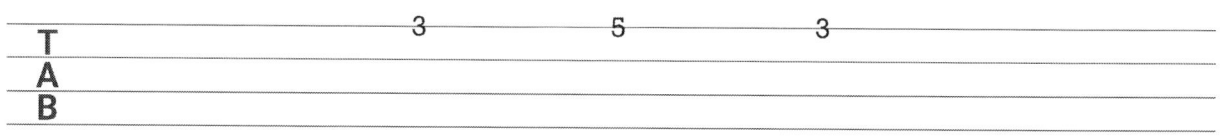

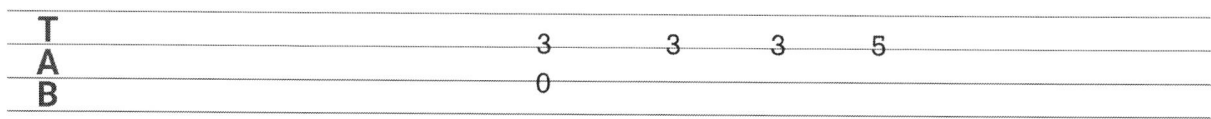

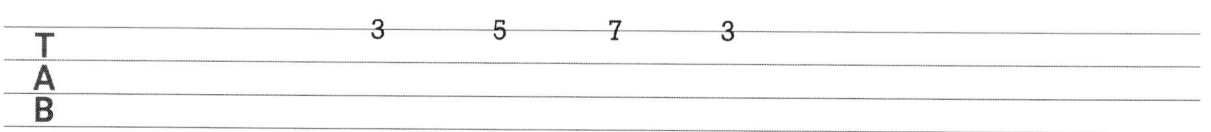

```
T |-----------5----7----5----3-----------|
A |-------------------------------------|
B |-------------------------------------|
```

```
T |-----------2----2----3----3-----------|
A |-------------------------------------|
B |-------------------------------------|
```

```
T |----------10---------10---12----------|
A |-----------0-------------------------|
B |-----------0-------------------------|
```

```
T |---------15--------15--------15--------10--------|
A |-------------------------------------|
B |-------------------------------------|
```

```
T |---------12--------15--------12--------|
A |-------------------------------------|
B |-------------------------------------|
```

```
T ――――――――――――――――――10――――――7――――――――
A ――――――――――――――――――――――――――――――――――
B ――――――――――――――――――――――――――――――――――


T ―――――――――7―――――――10―――――10―――――――
A ――――――――――――――――――――――――――――――――――
B ――――――――――――――――――――――――――――――――――


T ―――――――7―――7―――8―――7―――5―――――――――
A ――――――――――――――――――――――――――――――――――
B ――――――――――――――――――――――――――――――――――


T ―――――――5―――5―――7―――5―――3―――――――――
A ――――――――――――――――――――――――――――――――――
B ――――――――――――――――――――――――――――――――――


T ―――――――2―――2―――2―――2―――2―――――――――
A ――――――――――――――――――――――――――――――――――
B ――――――――――――――――――――――――――――――――――
```

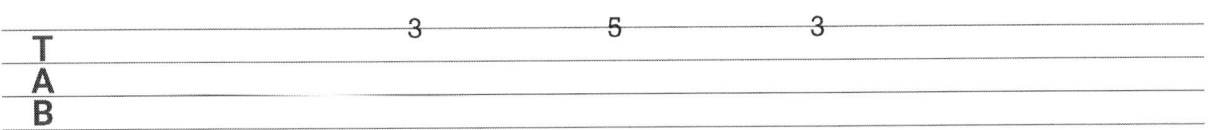

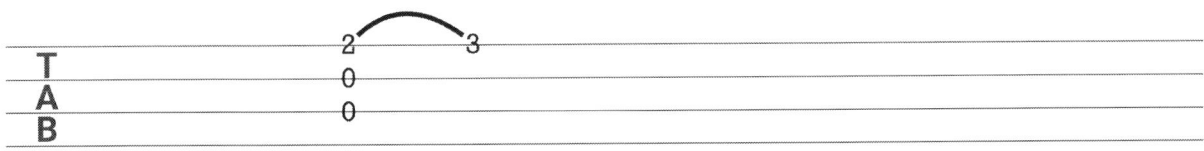

In Honour of St. Anne

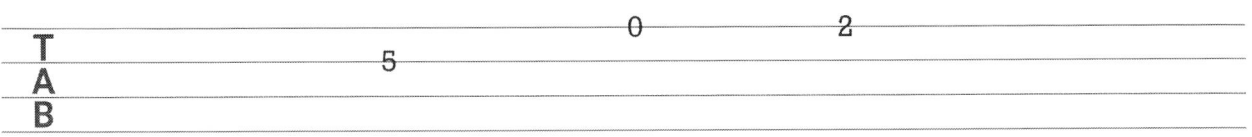

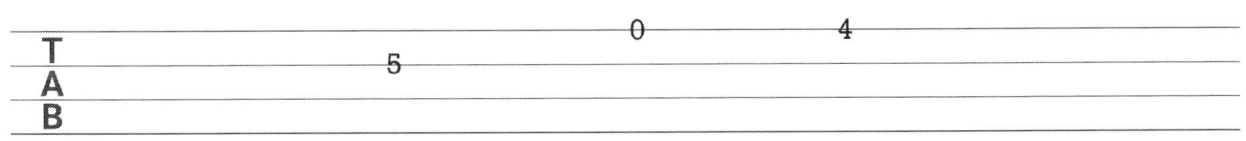

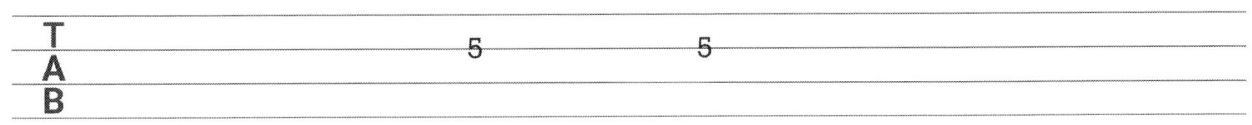

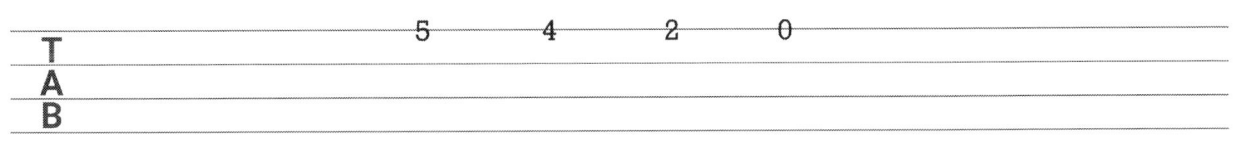

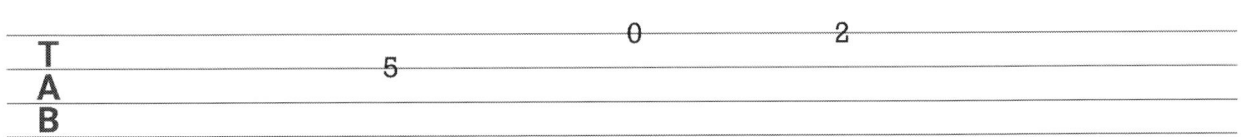

```
T|-----------------------------------0-------4-----------|
A|-------------5-----------------------------------------|
B|-------------------------------------------------------|


T|-------------------------5-----------5-----------------|
A|-------------------------------------------------------|
B|-------------------------------------------------------|


T|-----------------5-----4-----2-----0-------------------|
A|-------------------------------------------------------|
B|-------------------------------------------------------|


T|-------------------------------0-----2-----0-----------|
A|-------------5---------5-------------------------------|
B|-------------------------------------------------------|


T|-------------------------------------------------------|
A|-------------5-----5-----2-----0-----0-----------------|
B|-------------------------------------------------------|
```

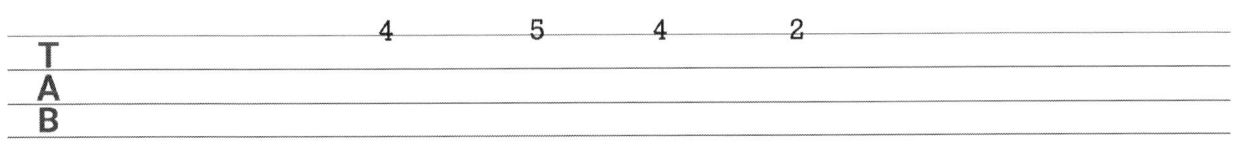
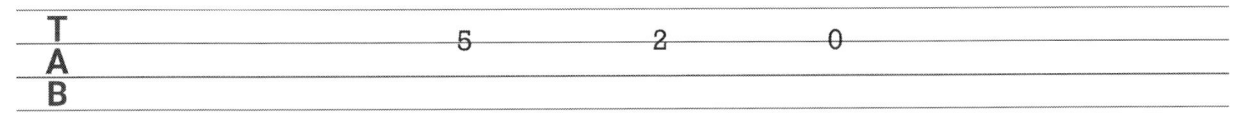
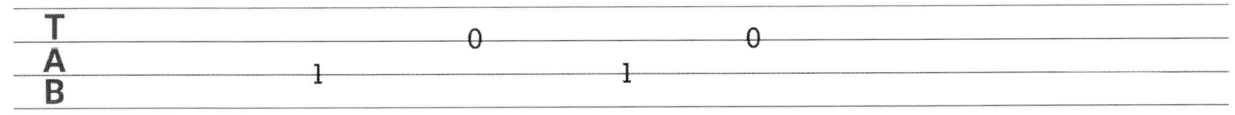

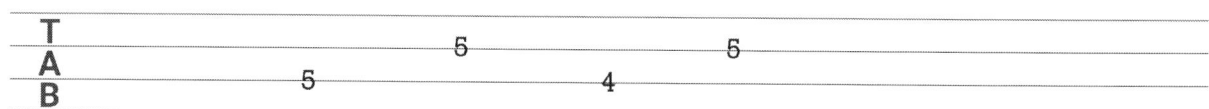

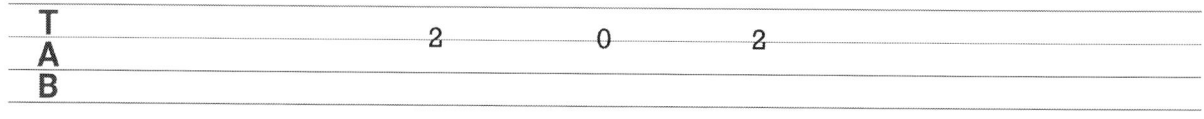

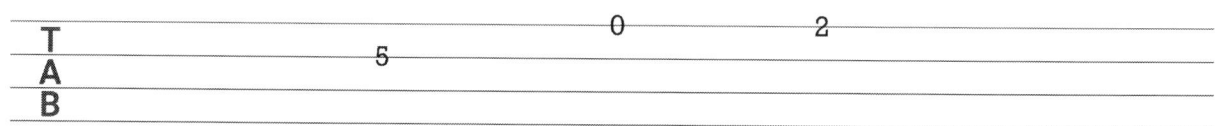

Relatively 'C'

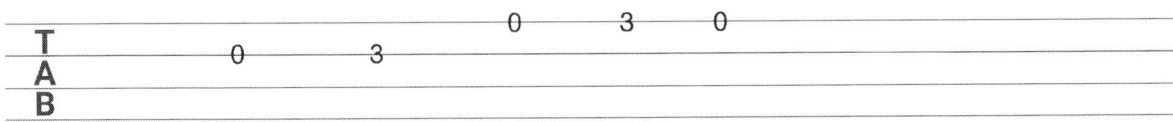

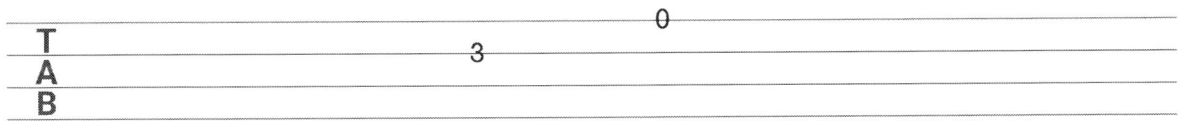

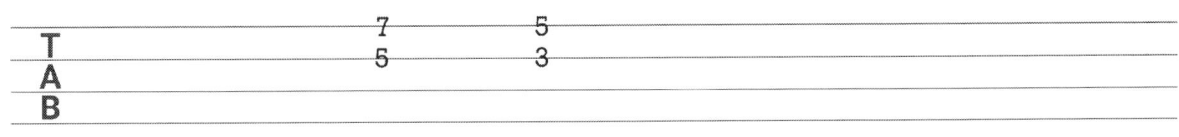

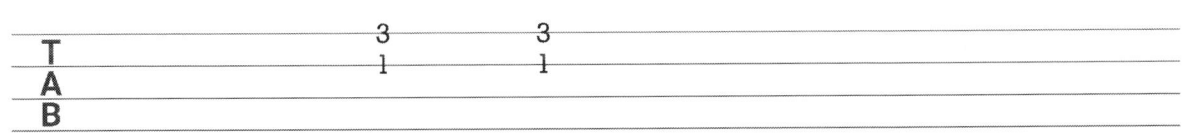

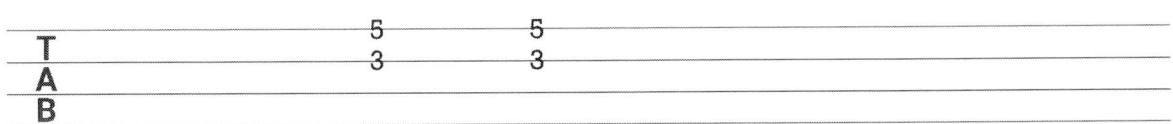

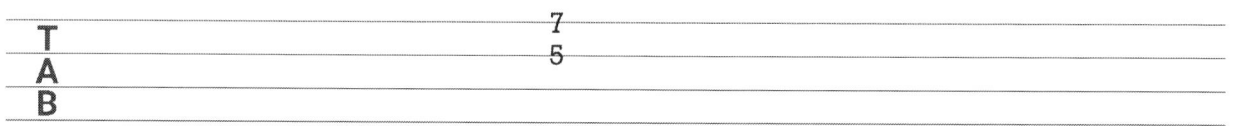

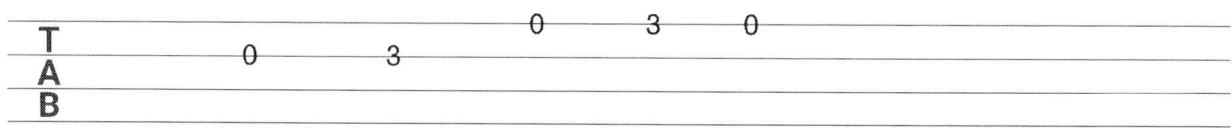

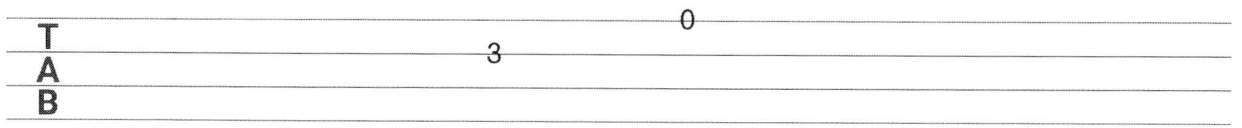

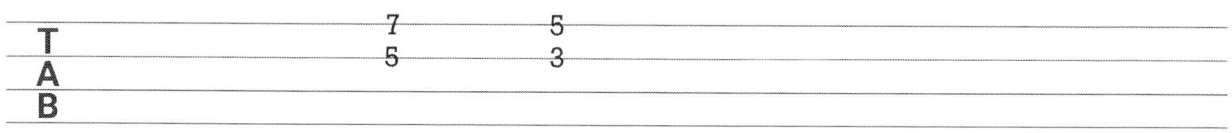

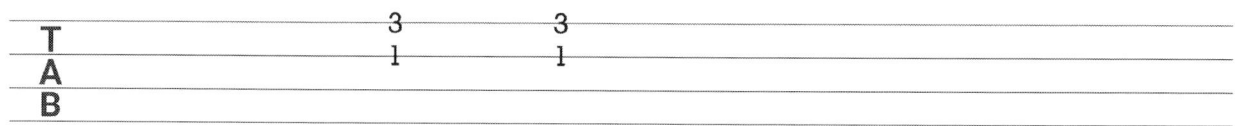

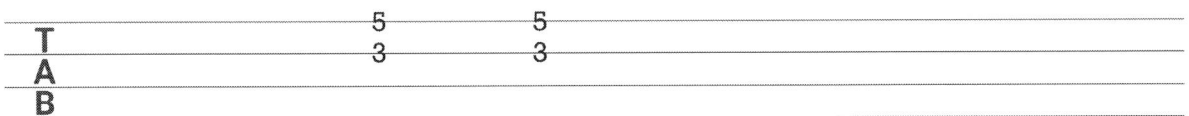

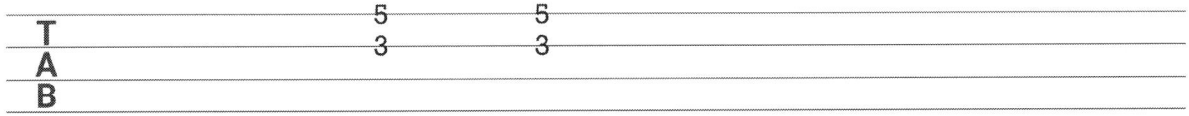

```
T|----------------5---------------|
A|----------------3---------------|
B|--------------------7-----------|
 |--------------------5-----------|
```

Night Life in NYC

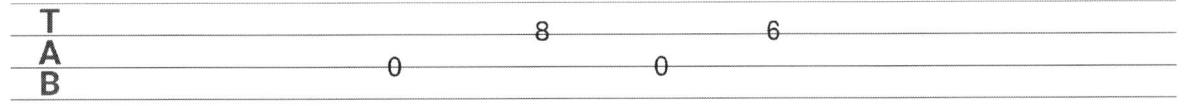

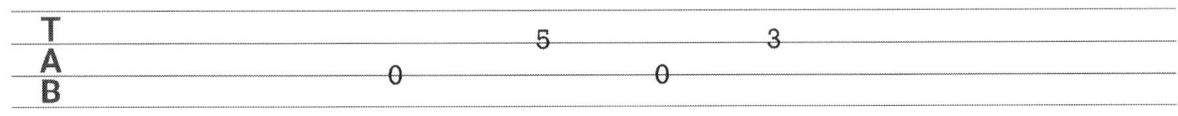

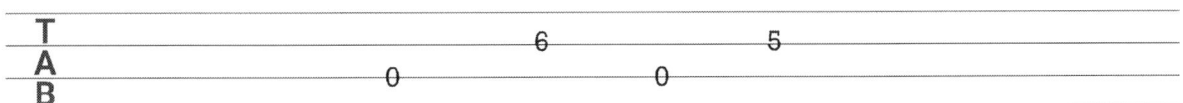

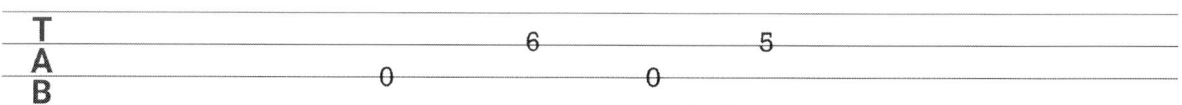

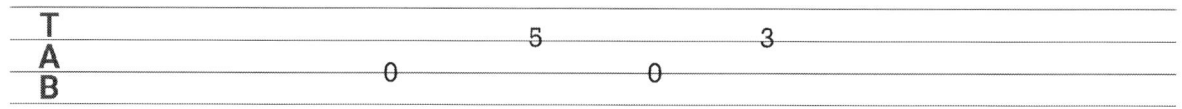

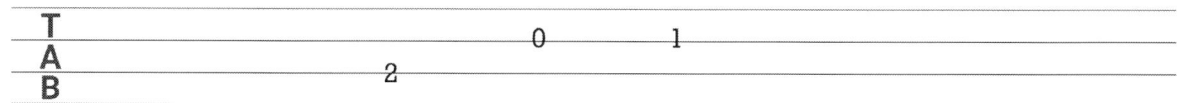

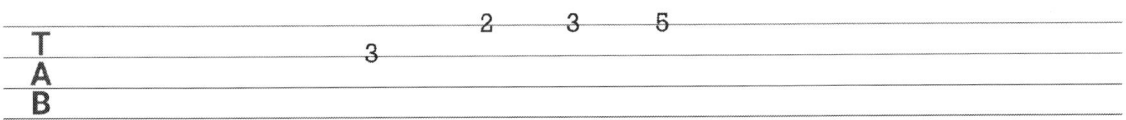

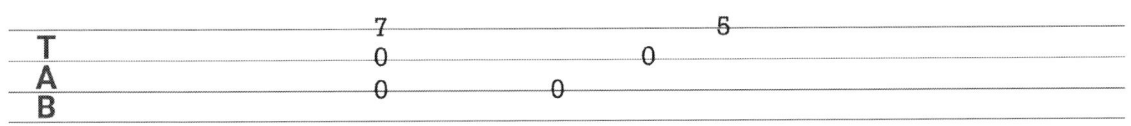

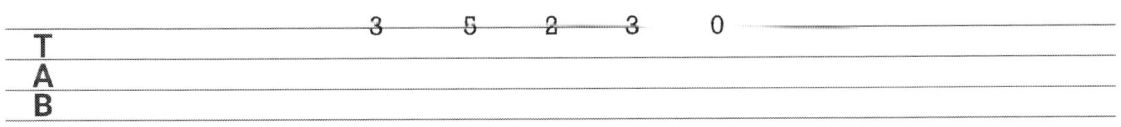

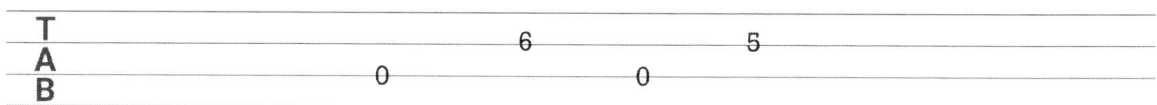

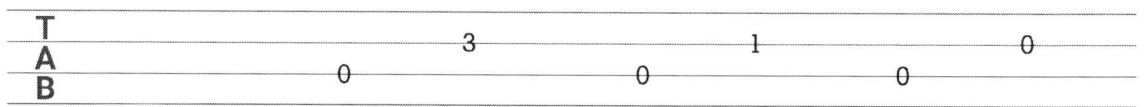

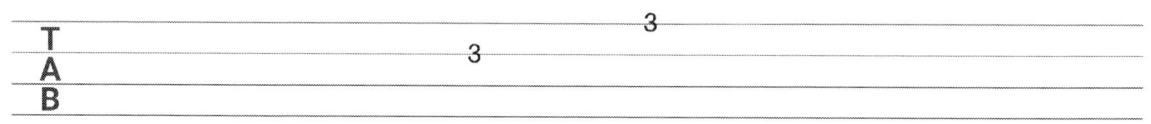

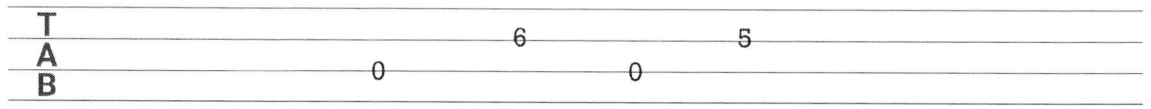

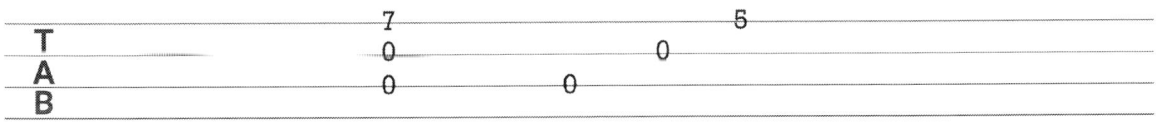

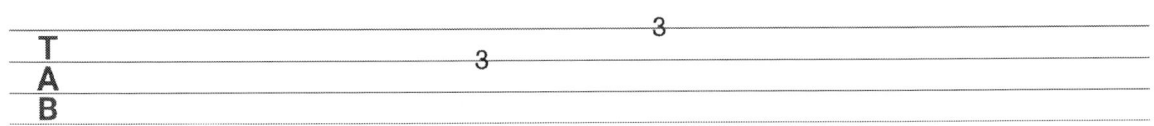

Amazing Grace
(Traditional Hymn)

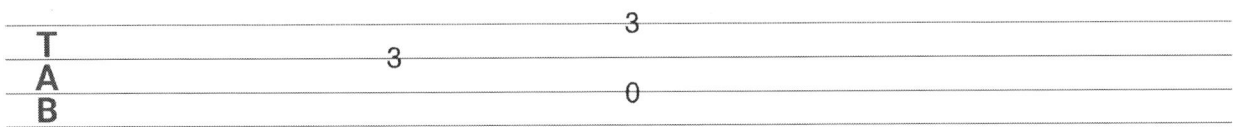

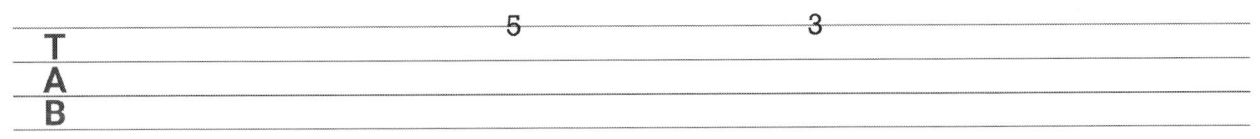

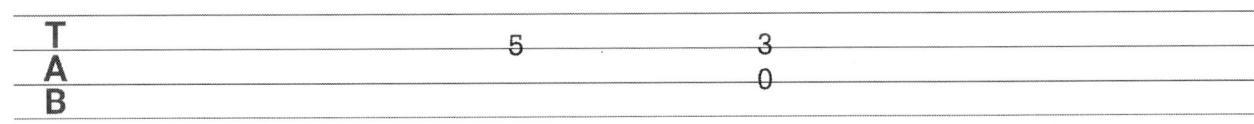

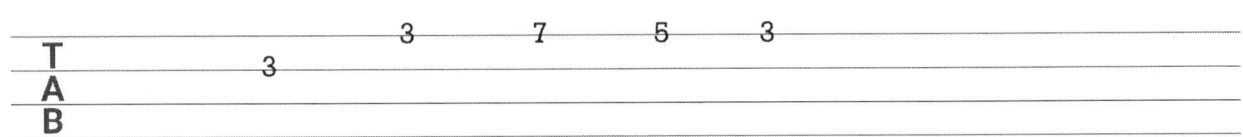

```
T ---------5-----7-----5-----------
A ----------------------------------
B ----------------------------------


T ---------------10----------------
A ----------------------------------
B ---------------0-----------------


T -------7------10-----10----------
A ----------------------------------
B --------------------0------------


T -------7---5---3---5---7---------
A ----------------------------------
B ----------------------------------


T -------5-------3-----------------
A ------------------3----5----3----
B ----------------------------------
```

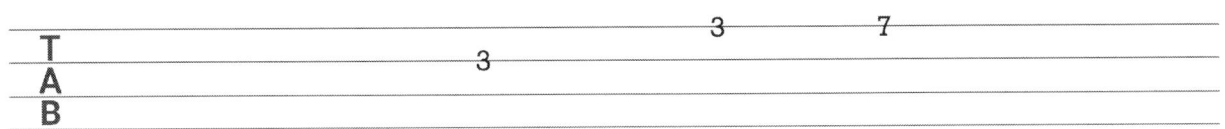

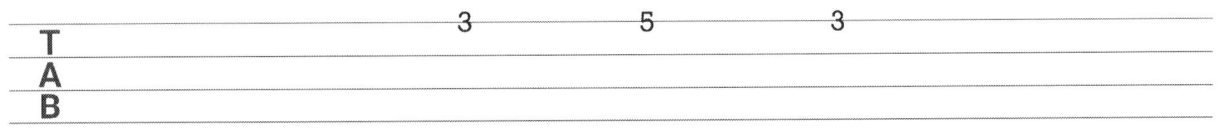

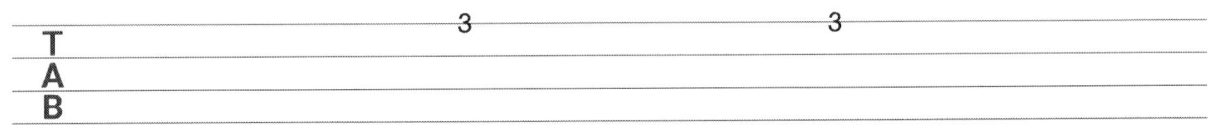

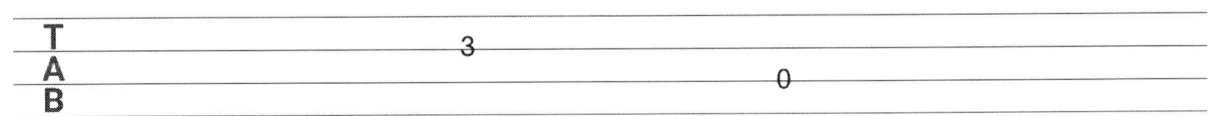

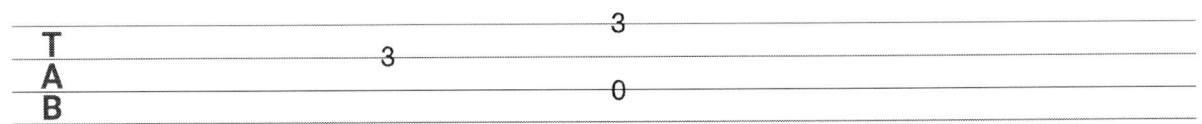

```
T|----------------7--5--3--5--7------------|
A|-----------------------------------------|
B|-----------------------------------------|


T|--------------5--------3-----------------|
A|-----------------------------------------|
B|-----------------------------------------|


T|--------------5--------3-----------------|
A|-----------------------------------------|
B|-----------------------0-----------------|


T|--------3--7--5--3-----------------------|
A|-----3-----------------------------------|
B|-----------------------------------------|


T|--------------5--7--5--------------------|
A|-----------------------------------------|
B|-----------------------------------------|
```

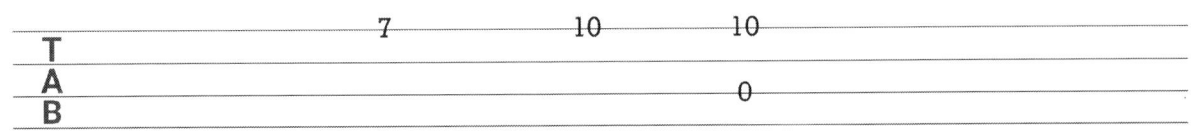

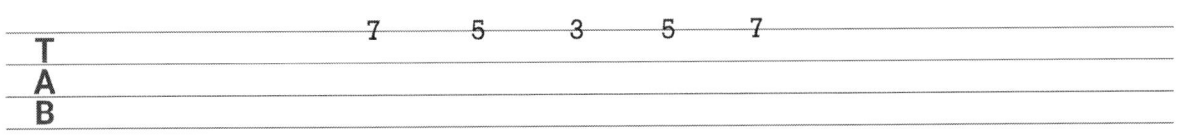

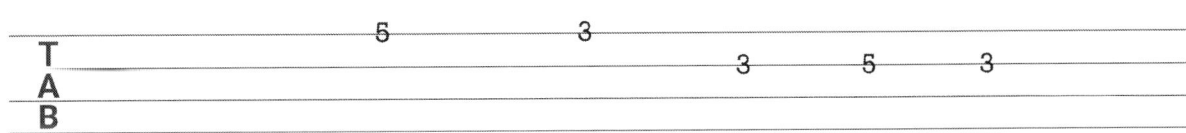

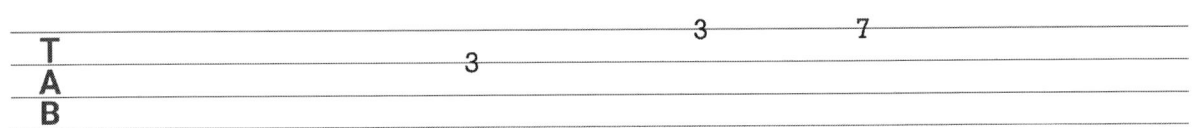

```
T|-------------------3-----------------3----------
A|-------------------------------------------------
B|-------------------------------------------------
```

```
T|-------------------------------------------------
A|-------------------3-----------------------------
B|-----------------------------------0-------------
```

Nothing to Give

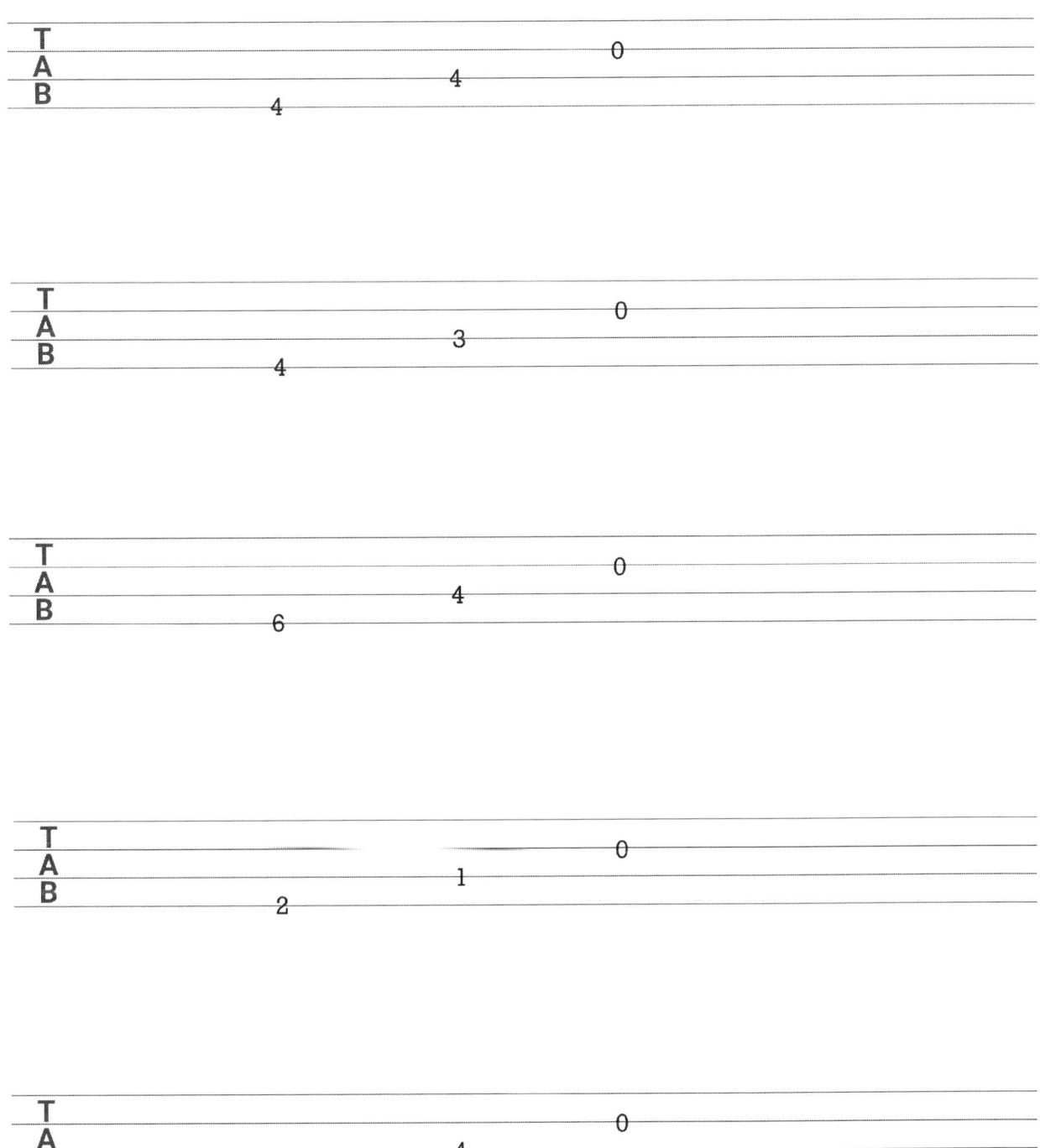

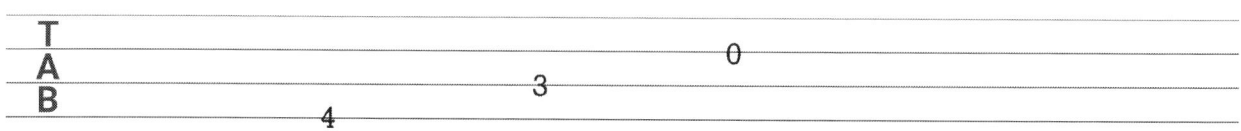
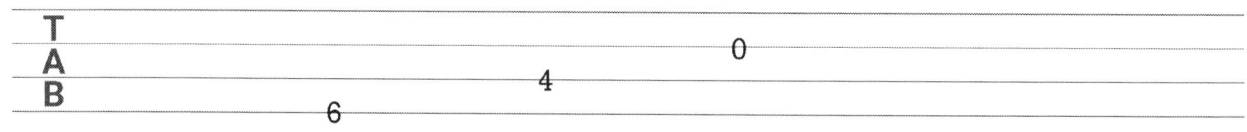
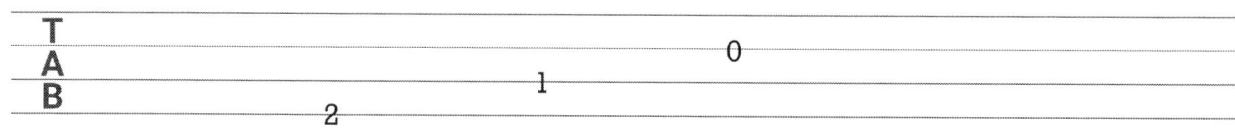

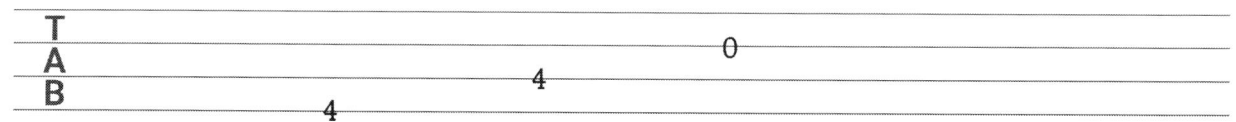

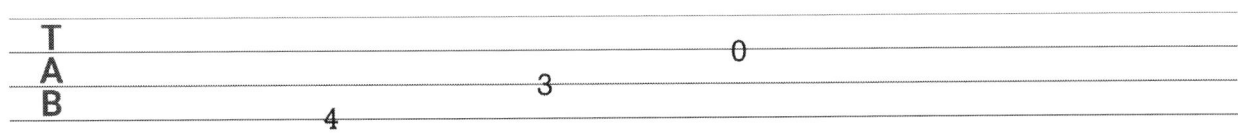
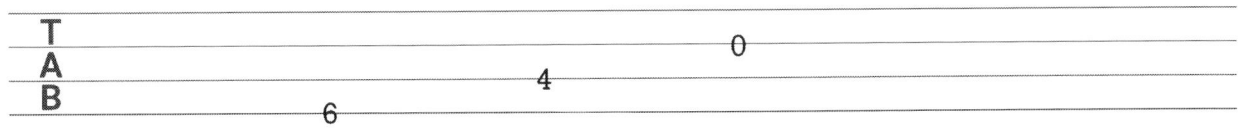
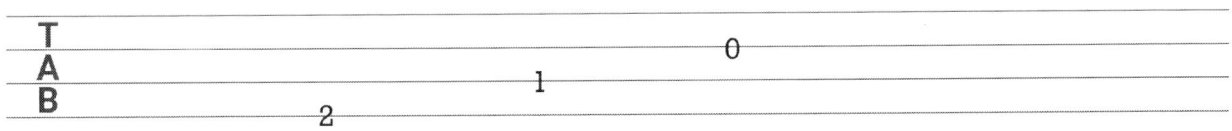
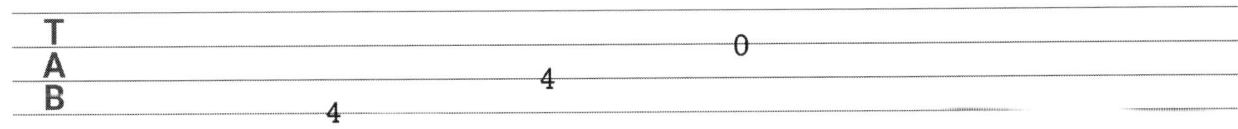
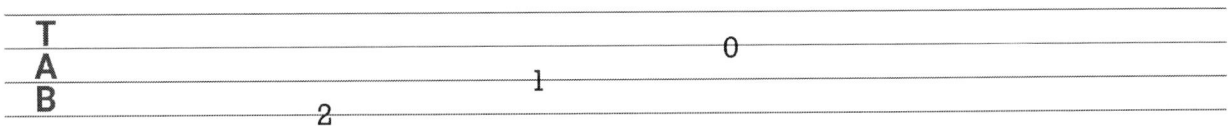

A Winter To Remember

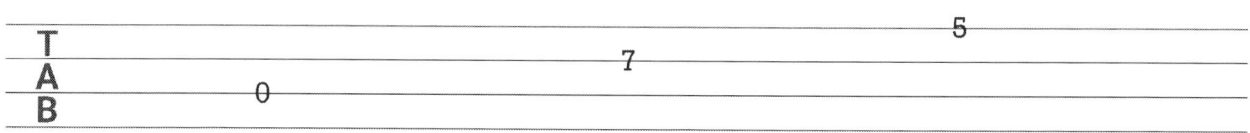
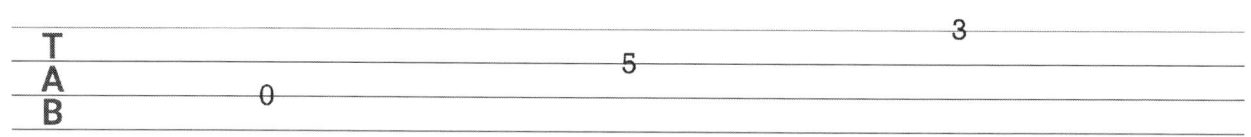
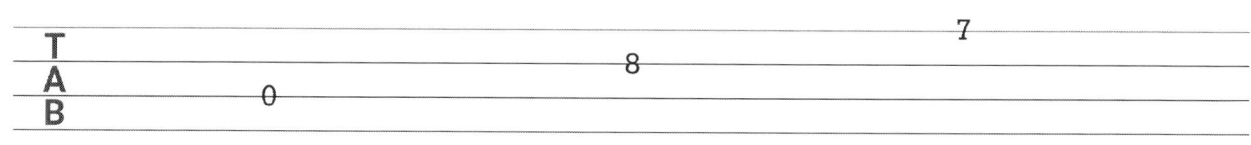
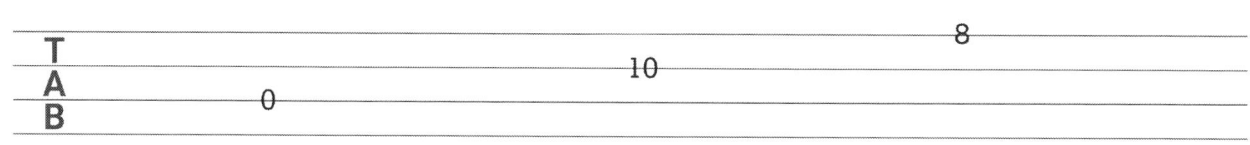
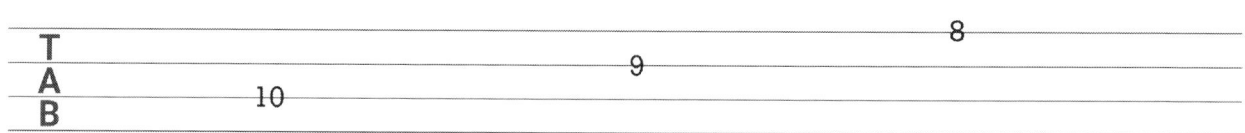

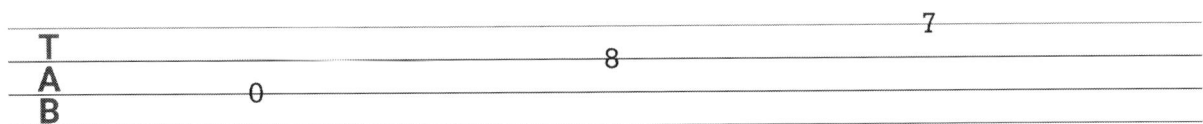

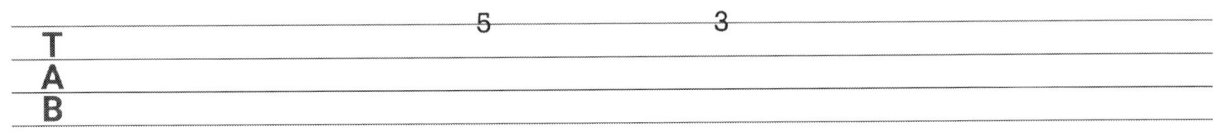

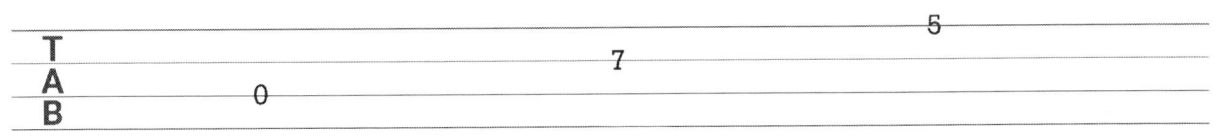

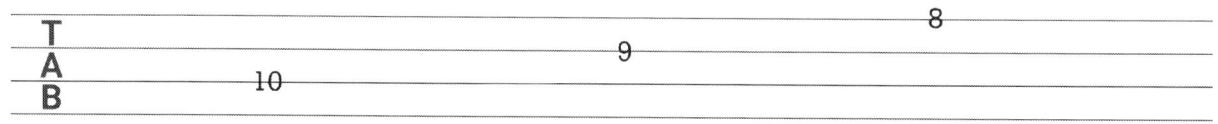

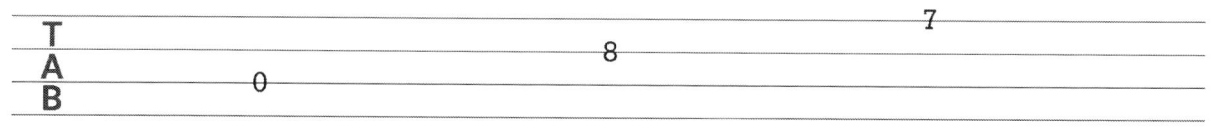

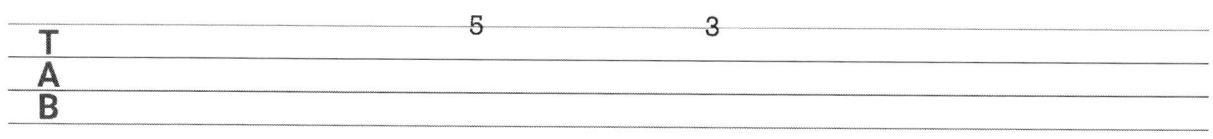

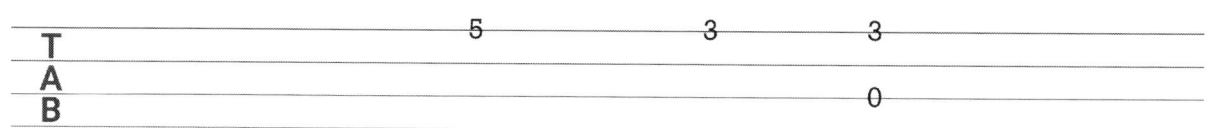

Printed in Great Britain
by Amazon